About the Book and Author

Dr. Laird provides the student of Soviet affairs, international security, and arms control with an understanding of the role of the Soviets in European security by examining the Soviet-French interaction. He first defines the general Soviet approach to European security issues and discusses it with specific reference to France. He identifies contemporary French perceptions of the Soviet challenge to Europe and analyzes French nuclear weapons deployments in the 1980s and 1990s and their impact on the European security environment. The impact of French policy on the Soviet approach to European security is discussed with specific reference to Soviet arms control policy. Dr. Laird concludes by summarizing the scope and nature of the Soviet-French interaction and analyzing the impact of this interaction on U.S. interests in Western Europe.

Dr. Robbin F. Laird is a member of the research staff of the Strategy, Forces, and Resources Division of the Institute for Defense Analyses. He is also an adjunct professor at Georgetown University and is affiliated with several professional organizations, including the Royal Institute of International Affairs, the International Institute for Strategic Studies, and the Institut Français des Relations Internationales. His publications include *The Soviet Union and Strategic Arms* (with Dale R. Herspring; Westview, 1984), *The Soviet Polity in the Modern Era* (1984), *Technocratic Socialism* (1985), and *Soviet Foreign Policy in a Changing World* (forthcoming).

Published in cooperation with
the Center for Naval Analyses

France, the Soviet Union, and the Nuclear Weapons Issue

Robbin F. Laird

Westview Press / Boulder and London

340918

Westview Special Studies in International Relations

Chapter 3 is reprinted from *Comparative Strategy* 4, 4 (1984), by permission of Crane, Russak & Company. Chapter 4 is reprinted from ORBIS: A Journal of World Affairs, Summer, 1984, by permission of the publisher.

Published in 1985 in the United States of America by Westview Press, Inc.; Frederick A. Praeger, Publisher; 5500 Central Avenue, Boulder, Colorado 80301

Library of Congress Cataloging in Publication Data
Laird, Robbin F. (Robbin Frederick), 1946–
    France, the Soviet Union, and the nuclear weapons issue.
    (Westview special studies in international relations)
    Bibliography: p.
    Includes index.
    1. France—Military policy.   2. Nuclear weapons—
France.   3. Soviet Union—Military policy. 4. Nuclear
weapons—Soviet Union. 5. Europe—Military policy.
6. Nuclear weapons—Europe. 7. North Atlantic Treaty
Organization. I. Title.
UA700.L35   1985   355'.033044   85-3304
ISBN 0-8133-7018-3

Printed and bound in the United States of America

10   9   8   7   6   5   4   3   2   1

To
Marie Hélène Chanier
and
Marie Claude de Saint-Hilarie

Contents

List of Tables and Figures

Tables

Figures

Preface

Three basic types of sources have been used in writing this book. First, French governmental and non-governmental publications on security issues were used to lay the foundation for the analysis of French security policy. Second, I conducted extensive interviews with members of the French security elite during frequent visits to France between 1980 and 1984. Third, a wide range of Russian-language materials was drawn upon to analyze the Soviet approach to European security issues and to determine specific Soviet perceptions of French security policy. All major Soviet publications dealing with France that have been issued since 1966 have been examined. Soviet monographs on French foreign and military policy have been analyzed as well as the more general Soviet politico-military literature, which contains significant discussions of French policy. All major Soviet foreign policy journals have been carefully examined, especially *Mirovaia ekonomika i mezhdunarodnye otnosheniia* (World Economy and International Relations), *Mezhdunarodnaia zhizn'* (International Affairs), and SShA (USA). Soviet military publications have also been consulted, notably, *Zarubezhnoe voennoe obozrenie* (Foreign Military Review), *Krasnaia zvezda* (Red Star), and *Morskoi sbornik* (Naval Digest).

Susan Clark and I translated the quotations from Russian-language sources. I translated all quotations from the French.

The combined use of original-language sources and interview data has provided a particularly difficult to obtain but fascinating blend of evidence. I hope that my effort in studying Soviet and West European security issues not in isolation from one another but in their inter-action will encourage others along the same path.

This book could not have been written without the support of many colleagues. A number of people contributed to the evolution of my thinking on European security issues. I especially wish to thank Carl

Bernard, Greg Flynn, Robert Gelbard, Michael Harrison, Pierre Hassner, Joseph Joffe, Jean Klein, Christopher Makins, Harold Malmgren, J. Robert Schaetzel, and Samuel Wells in this regard. Similarly, I wish to thank Alexander Arnot, Zbigniew Brzezinski, Renata Fritsch-Bournazel, William Garner, Dale Herspring, Erik Hoffmann, Mark Palmer, and Angela Stent for their general contributions to my thinking about Soviet security issues.

A number of persons contributed specifically to the successful completion of the book. Robin Pirie was instrumental in seeing the project initiated. Susan Clark contributed absolutely critical research assistance of the finest quality. As always, Della Smith provided timely and superb typing support. Karen Domabyl provided skillful editorial support in seeing the project through to completion. Charles Petersen, Brad Dismukes, James George, and James McConnell made helpful comments on various drafts.

Quite literally, the project could not have been contemplated, let alone completed, without the intellectual and infrastructural support of the Institut Français des Relations Internationales. I would like to thank all of my IFRI colleagues for their help. My work began in 1980 through the mediation of my friendship with the late Marc Gilbert, whose loss will always be deeply felt by me. Thierry de Montbrial, director of IFRI, gave me assistance throughout the project. Marie Hélène Chanier and Marie Claude de Saint Hilarie provided me with critical logistical support during my various stays in Paris. It is in recognition of their efforts on my behalf that I have dedicated this book to them.

In addition, I would like to acknowledge the permission of Crane, Russak and Co. to republish my article, "French Nuclear Forces in the 1980s and 1990s," from *Comparative Strategy* 4 (1984), 387-412. I would also like to thank the Foreign Policy Research Institute for permission to republish my article, "The French Strategic Dilemma," from *Orbis: A Journal of World Affairs* 28 (Summer 1984), 307-328. Finally, it should be noted that this book does not necessarily represent the views of either the Center for Naval Analyses or the Department of Defense.

Robbin F. Laird

Introduction

Rarely has a crisis in East-West relations been more analyzed or debated than NATO's decision to deploy new medium-range American nuclear missiles in Europe. In December 1979, NATO agreed to the U.S. deployment of 108 Pershing II missiles and 464 ground-launched cruise missiles (GLCMs) in Europe. Scheduled deployment began in November 1983, to be completed by 1988. The systems are under American control, although located on NATO European territory.

At the time of the public announcement of the decision, Britain, West Germany, and Italy committed themselves to the deployment of the new missiles on their territory. Britain agreed to the basing of 160 GLCMs, West Germany to 108 Pershing IIs and 96 GLCMs, and Italy to 112 GLCMs. The Netherlands and Belgium agreed with the deployment in principle but did not publicly commit themselves to basing the missiles on their territory.

NATO's December 1979 decision was a "two-track" or "double" decision in that it included a commitment to try to negotiate with the Soviets in order to stabilize the theater nuclear balance at the lowest possible level. The West would use the Pershing IIs and GLCMs in part as bargaining chips to induce the Soviets to negotiate reductions on their SS-20, SS-4, and SS-5 intermediate-range ballistic missiles (IRBMs).

The NATO decision had its origin in the military and political challenges confronting the Western Alliance. During the mid-1970s, NATO officials became increasingly apprehensive about the growing capabilities of Soviet intermediate-range nuclear forces (INFs). The Backfire bomber and the SS-20 IRBM, which were being deployed at that time, seemed to signal a Soviet willingness to try to circumvent the SALT agreements. These new Soviet weapons were not included in the U.S.-Soviet SALT negotiations, and seemed to West European leaders to pose an especially direct threat to their interests. If the Soviet Union could develop a large and modern intermediate-range force threatening only West European territory and not limited by U.S.-Soviet agreements, the Soviets could dramatically erode the American nuclear guarantee. West European leaders, especially in West Germany, France, and Britain, saw a need for a military and diplomatic response to the new Soviet systems that would reconfirm the American guarantee.

A key crystallization of the West European position was a major speech by West German Chancellor Helmut Schmidt in 1977. Schmidt openly expressed concern with the credibility of the American nuclear guarantee to Europe.

> SALT neutralizes [the U.S. and Soviet] strategic nuclear capabilities. In Europe this magnifies the significance of the disparities between East and West in nuclear tactical and conventional weapons....
>
> It is of vital interest to us all that the negotiations between the two super-powers on the limitation and reduction of nuclear strategic weapons should continue and lead to a lasting agreement. The nuclear powers have a special, an overwhelming responsibility in this field. On the other hand, we in Europe must be particularly careful to ensure that these negotiations do not neglect the components of NATO's deterrence strategy.
>
> We are all faced with the dilemma of having to meet the moral and political demand for arms limitation while at the same time maintaining a fully effective deterrent to war. We are not unaware that both the United States and the Soviet Union must be anxious to remove threatening strategic developments from their relationship. But strategic arms limitations confined to the United States and the Soviet Union will inevitably impair the security of the West European members of the Alliance *vis-a-vis* Soviet military superiority in Europe if we do not succeed in removing the disparities of military power in Europe parallel to the SALT negotiations. So long as this is not the case we must maintain the balance of the full range of deterrence strategy. The Alliance must, therefore, be ready to make available the means to support its present strategy, which is still the right one, and to prevent any developments that could undermine the basis of this strategy.[1]

The thrust of Schmidt's remarks was to underscore the significance of a U.S.-Soviet "Eurostrategic" imbalance. According to David Schwartz, Schmidt was implying, in contrast to NATO policy over the previous 20 years, that

> somehow the balance of military forces in the European theater could be considered separately from the overall military balance between the two blocs. By implication, therefore, the statement seemed to be questioning the ability of U.S. forces outside the theater---especially the strategic nuclear forces--to deter conflict in Europe and expressing the fear that parity achieved in strategic nuclear arsenals through SALT might make the theater nuclear balance, the so-called Eurostrategic balance, more important.[2]

The military rationale for deploying new U.S. INF systems rested upon the need to "recouple" U.S. intercontinental systems with INF systems. The Soviet INF deployments, by threatening West European, but not American, territory, served to "decouple" in the sense of allowing the Soviets the possibility of fighting a nuclear war limited to Europe. The main thrust of the coupling argument was tacitly, not explicitly, made. Leon Sigal has provided a clear formulation of the tacit military rationale for the American Euromissiles.

> An alternative rationale acknowledges the vulnerability of NATO's new missiles to Soviet nuclear preemption but regards that vulnerability as potentially helpful in deterring conventional war in Europe. Prudent Soviet planners, uncertain whether these weapons would be used against their homeland in the course of a war in Europe, would have to eliminate them. If GLCMs and Pershing IIs could be rendered invulnerable to other than nuclear attack, then Soviet planners would have to employ nuclear weapons. In so doing they would also have to contemplate striking first at U.S. strategic nuclear forces, thereby putting the United States as well as the European basing countries at risk. In this sense the deployment would reinforce coupling of the American deterrent to European security. And by forcing Soviet leaders to consider initiating use of nuclear weapons as part of any attack on Europe, it would increase immeasurably the risk associated with that attack, a risk they might not care to assume. European-based missiles would thus contribute to deterring the Soviet Union from starting any war.[3]

With a growing sense of the need to deal with the INF problem, NATO's Nuclear Planning Group (NPG) in the fall of 1977 established a special High Level Group (HLG) to study the matter. Normally, the staff of the NPG provides studies directly for the NPG. In this case, the establishment of the HLG provided a mechanism for the involvement of high-ranking national decision-makers because such involvement was critical to developing a resolution to the political dimensions of the INF problem.

The HLG and the NATO defense ministers developed a consensus around the need to develop a credible long-range nuclear capability on European territory, and in the spring of 1978, NATO tasked the United States to study the deployment options. This study suggested that the only real choices open to NATO were the deployment of the Pershing II ballistic missile and a ground-launched cruise missile.

Based on this recommendation, the HLG proceeded to evaluate the basing modes. Eventually, the arguments in favor of land-based systems prevailed. A persuasive argument for land-based systems was the political necessity to deploy weapons with very high visibility symbolically. Land-based systems promised to more visibly demonstrate to the Soviet Union, as well as to West European publics, that the American nuclear guarantee to Western Europe was being reinforced.

During the deliberations of the HLG, it gradually became apparent that arms control would be an inextricable component of NATO's approach to the INF issue. The NPG appointed a Special Group to study the arms control task. One of the major questions that the Special Group took up was the timing of negotiations with the Soviet Union. It was felt that a deployment decision should precede negotiations. A decision to deploy new NATO INF systems was needed to induce the Soviet Union to negotiate, because the Soviets were already strengthening their INFs in the absence of NATO action. It was felt, however, to be politically necessary not to postpone the offer to negotiate until after the decision to deploy, lest Western public opinion consider NATO to be needlessly escalating the arms race. The idea for two simultaneous decisions, or a "double-track" decision, arose from the sense of need to show resolve to deploy but willingness to reduce the INF threat through negotiations.

The recommendations of the High Level Group and the Special Group were ratified at an NPG meeting in November 1979. The final communique of this meeting underscored the need for both arms control and arms modernization.

Ministers reaffirmed that modernization and arms control negotiations involving long-range theater nuclear forces should be complementary ways of achieving the fundamental aim of maintaining and improving Alliance security and of enhancing overall stability and detente. In this context, the Ministers welcomed the constructive preparations of arms control proposals designed to engage the Soviet Union in negotiations aimed at reducing the disparity in the level of nuclear forces, thus furthering the maintenance of peace with undiminished security.[4]

The recommendations of the NPG were ratified by the NATO Council on 12 December 1979. Unfortunately, the process envisaged in the NATO decision proved to be a rocky one at best. The tensions of the predeployment period (1979-83) created a sense of crisis in West-West and East-West relations. The Western analytical literature has dealt with virtually all dimensions of this so-called Euromissile crisis. Some analysts have focused on the West-West dimension of the Euromissile issue.[5] Others have concentrated on the U.S.-Soviet competition in intermediate-range nuclear weapons.[6] Still others have analyzed Soviet motivations and concerns evident in the crisis.[7]

This book deals with a neglected, yet critical, dimension of the Euromissile issue, namely the conflict between the Soviet Union and France over the role of nuclear weapons in European defense. The

Soviets throughout the Euromissile crisis have hoped to "denuclearize" Europe, to exacerbate U.S.-West European tensions, and to forestall trends toward greater West European independence associated with the evolution of the British and French nuclear forces. In contrast, the French have sought to bolster the legitimacy of the role of nuclear weapons in the defense of Europe, to strengthen the American-West European nuclear connection, and to enhance West European cooperation in the security field.

The underlying argument of this book is that Soviet behavior in the Euromissile crisis, in particular, and on the broader question of the enhancement of Western Europe's nuclear capability is motivated by concern that a stronger Western Europe, more independent and more capable of defending itself, might well be emerging. The Soviets hope to promote, or at least contribute to, a crisis of statecraft in the West and thereby impede the development of a more "mature" partnership between Western Europe and the United States. The Soviets hope to contribute to the decline of Atlanticism without encouraging the further development of West European cooperation in economic, political, and military areas. They are especially concerned to impede the emergence of a better division of labor between Western Europe and the United States in the security area, a division that would allow the Americans to confront the Soviet Union more effectively both within and outside Europe.

The Soviets are having to come to terms with an increasingly assertive Western Europe. Especially significant to the Soviets is the need to influence the shape and direction of West European foreign policy as the West struggles to define its policy in East-West relations. The increased assertiveness of Western Europe provides the Soviets with opportunities to undercut American influence in Western Europe and to try to hinder the development of various kinds of Western relationships that the Soviets find damaging to their interests. The Soviet objective is to reduce the room for maneuver, or the margins of permissible error, in Western security policies.

This book is structured so that the analysis of the Soviet-French conflict over the Euromissile issue leads to a broader discussion of the conflicting interests served by Soviet and French nuclear weapons in Europe. This discussion, in turn, leads to an understanding of more general Soviet objectives in Europe and in East-West relations. The first chapter deals with the conflicting assessments made by the Soviet Union and France during the Euromissile crisis (1979-1984). The second chapter covers the military and political roles served by Soviet nuclear weapons in the European theater. The third and fourth chapters provide a description and analysis of the military and political roles served by French nuclear weapons. The fifth and final chapter gives an overview of how Soviet political and military analysts have characterized the scope, nature, and challenge of French security policy. By understanding Soviet perspectives on the challenges and opportunities posed by the evolution of French security policy, one is able to gain a sense of the Soviet concern with the trend toward greater independence within Western Europe on security matters.

Notes

1. Helmut Schmidt, "The 1977 Alastair Buchan Memorial Lecture," *Survival* 20 (January/February 1978): 3-4.

2. David N. Schwartz, *NATO's Nuclear Dilemmas* (Washington, D.C.: Brookings Institution, 1983), 215.

3. Leon V. Sigal, *Nuclear Forces in Europe: Enduring Dilemmas, Present Prospects* (Washington, D.C.: Brookings Institution, 1984), 47.

4. "Documentation," *NATO Review,* December 1979, 28.

5. See, for example, William Hyland, "The Struggle for Europe: An American View," in *Nuclear Weapons in Europe*, ed. Andrew J. Pierre (New York: Council on Foreign Relations, 1984), 15-44.

6. See, for example, Jed C. Snyder, "European Security, East-West Policy, and the INF Debate," *Orbis* 28 (Winter 1984): 913-970.

7. See, for example, William V. Garner, *Soviet Threat Perceptions of NATO's Eurostrategic Missiles* (Paris: Atlantic Institute for International Affairs, 1983).

1

The Soviet Union, France, and the Eurostrategic Issue, 1979-1984

This chapter describes the Soviet and French responses to NATO's decision to deploy American Euromissiles. It then contrasts the Soviet and French positions and analyzes their diverging interests in the Euromissile crisis.

The Soviet Union and NATO's "Double Decision"

Before NATO's December 1979 decision to deploy U.S. intermediate-range nuclear forces (INFs) in Europe, the Soviets waged an intensive propaganda and political campaign in an attempt to stop the modernization decision from being taken. The Soviets portrayed the proposed decision as unjustified and aggressive. They proposed in October 1979 to remove 20,000 Soviet troops from the German Democratic Republic and offered to negotiate on a mutual reduction of INF systems. Nonetheless, this proposal was conditional on NATO's not taking a decision to deploy new U.S. INFs.

After the December decision was made, the Soviets initially insisted that talks on INFs could be held only if the decision was revoked. The Soviets maintained that a balance already existed between NATO and Soviet INFs in Europe. The proposed U.S. deployment would upset the balance. They therefore insisted that any talks must include all Western nuclear systems of medium range, on land and at sea, including those under British and French control. Marshal Kulikov made clear the Soviet position:

U.S. "experts" are resorting to the most varied tricks to prove the completely unfounded assertion about the USSR's upsetting the balance of power. Thus, for example, they omit in their calculations the U.S. forward-based nuclear means...and also ignore the nuclear weapons of other NATO states that could hit the territory of the USSR and its allies. We, however, must include the aforementioned means in our calculations because they are aimed at the Soviet Union and the states of the socialist community. They constitute the basis of NATO's nuclear potential in Europe. If one wished to make an objective judgment when calculating the balance of power, individual types of weapons must not be studied in isolation from one another but the nuclear potential of both sides must be compared as a whole, and this potential now is approximately equal.[1]

The Soviets are especially concerned to protect their Eurostrategic capability, for these systems potentially enable the Soviets to neutralize NATO nuclear forces in the event of hostilities. Consequently, even a partial U.S. INF modernization program has been perceived by Moscow as a threat to the existing "balance" and hence damaging to Soviet interests. As Boris Ponomarev has underscored,

When the West began to draw up the "new nuclear strategy" and the program for manufacturing new missiles to be added to existing medium-range facilities, it was a threat to the parity of forces in Europe. In these conditions, the modernization of Soviet medium-range missiles does not make any essential change to the strategic situation, to the balance of forces on the continent, and does not destroy existing parity. It is merely that some facilities are replaced by others, which are less powerful but more accurate. However, both [the old and new Soviet IRBMs] have the same objective: to balance the forward-based nuclear facilities in Europe or nearby....[2]

Nonetheless, the Soviets have been anxious to appear willing to negotiate, in part as a propaganda weapon in the struggle for public opinion in the West, and in order to prevent or to delay significantly the U.S. INF deployment. To this end, the Soviets have portrayed themselves as more genuinely concerned with European security than the United States. As Brezhnev stated in 1981,

The U.S. planned deployment in Western Europe of new U.S. missiles targeted on the Soviet Union and its allies is presented as a measure to protect European NATO countries. In actual fact this is an attempt to tilt in favor of the American side the strategic balance established by the SALT treaty between the USSR and the United States. At the same time, in case of a conflict the vulnerability of West European countries will of course grow to a great extent. In the meantime the interests of all peoples call for the continuation of the SALT process and the resumption of corresponding negotiations. The Soviet Union is ready to start such negotiations.[3]

During November 1981, American and Soviet leaders made public proposals for the reduction of INFs, which were based on very different assessments of the INF balance. For the United States, the deployment of the new systems was necessary to restore parity; for the Soviets, deployment upset parity.

In his speech at the National Press Club on 18 November 1981, President Reagan said that "the United States is prepared to cancel its deployment of Pershing II and ground-launched cruise missiles if the Soviets will dismantle their SS-20, SS-4, and SS-5 missiles." Only with the complete elimination of these Soviet missiles would parity be restored. This "zero option" proposal included a requirement that all Soviet missiles of these types be dismantled regardless of their location, including those deployed in the Soviet Far East. The U.S. was concerned that the mobility of the SS-20 meant that moving the missiles out of the European theater would lead to their deployment or storage elsewhere.

Brezhnev asserted during his trip to West Germany in November 1981 that a theater nuclear balance already existed. During an address in Bonn on 24 November, the Soviet leader proposed that if the United States was prepared to accept a moratorium on deployment, the Soviets would not only be ready to halt the deployment of the SS-20s, but would be ready unilaterally to reduce the number of missiles in the European part of the Soviet Union. As part of an agreement the Soviets would be prepared to make substantial reductions in European theater nuclear weapons. In Brezhnev's words, Europe should become free of "all kinds of medium-range nuclear systems directed towards Europe...as well as of tactical weapons. That would be a real 'zero option.'" In light of the increasing emphasis placed in Soviet military thought and force structure on a conventional warfighting option in Europe, it is not inconceivable that Brezhnev was making a serious proposal. The result of such an agreement would be, of course, to place Europe under the shadow of the threat of Soviet conventional military power.

From the American point of view, shown in table 1.1, the Soviets already had a six-to-one lead in European INFs. In terms of intermediate-range ballistic missiles (IRBMs), the United States calculated that the Soviets had 700 (including the SS-12 Scaleboard), to none for the United States. In terms of submarine-launched ballistic missiles (SLBMs), the Soviets had some 30 SS-N-5s deployed on Hotel-class submarines that were not counted under the SALT agreements. In contrast, American SLBMs dedicated to European theater missions had already been counted in the SALT agreements. More controversially, in assessing the theater aircraft balance, the United States counted all of the potentially nuclear-capable

TABLE 1.1
U.S. VIEW, NOVEMBER 1981:
USSR LEADS BY 6 TO 1

	INFs in the European Theater	
Type	U.S.	USSR
IRBMs	0	250 SS-20 350 SS-4/5 100 SS-12/22
SLBMs	0	30 SS-N-5
Bombers	164 F-111 in W. Europe 63 FB-111 in U.S. 265 F-4 68 A-6/7	45 Backfire 350 Blinder, Badger 2,700 Su-17, Su-24, MiG 27
Total	560	3,825

tactical aircraft in the Soviet inventory directed at Europe, as well as theater bombers. No West European nuclear forces were counted.

From the Soviet point of view, shown in table 1.2, a balance of NATO and Soviet INFs already existed. In terms of IRBMs, the Soviets excluded their SS-12/22s but included the 18 French IRBMs. The Soviets also counted the 64 British and 80 French SLBMs. They included all U.S. aircraft based on carriers and British and French bombers, while excluding all of the Soviet tactical inventory. Most significantly, the Soviets included non-U.S. systems.

The U.S. and Soviet calculations reflect different strategic assessments. The United States has been concerned to make the NATO strategy of flexible response more credible by deploying a missile system that more effectively couples European and American forces. The British and French systems simply cannot play the same role as do the U.S. missile systems in implementing flexible response.

For the Soviets, the U.S. Euromissiles are strategic, not theater, forces. (For a general Soviet perspective on the INF issue, see the

TABLE 1.2
SOVIET VIEW, NOVEMBER 1981:
USSR AND NATO IN BALANCE

Type	INFs in the European Theater	
	U.S. + NATO	USSR
IRBMs	18 French	243 SS-20
		253 SS-4/5
SLBMs	80 French	18 SS-N-5
	64 British	
Bombers	172 U.S. F-111	461 Backfire, Blinder,
	65 U.S. FB-111	Badger
	246 U.S. F-4	
	240 U.S. A-6/7	
	46 French Mirage IVA	
	55 British Vulcan	
Total	986	975

selection from A. Arbatov in appendix A.) The new missiles give
the United States more flexibility to implement a war-winning
strategy. These missiles allow the United States to destroy Soviet
military targets without using systems based on American territory.
In addition, the British and French systems must be included because
of their increasing military significance. Also, if the United States
could be forced to take into account these strictly national strategic
forces, the Soviets would hope to undercut the political rationale in
Britain and France for having an independent nuclear deterrent at
all.

There is an important contradiction in Soviet thinking about the
character of European theater nuclear weapons. For the Soviets, U.S.
INFs are strategic in character, whereas Soviet INFs are not. Defense
Minister Ustinov has articulated the Soviet position as follows:

The new American medium-range missiles are strategic weapons with regard to
the Soviet Union.... While declaring officially that the new missiles are allegedly
meant for the defense of West European countries, Washington in actual fact is

intending to use them for preventive strikes on Soviet ICBMs and other vitally important installations situated in the Western areas of the USSR. After all, the Pershing II missiles, which possess a range of 2,500 kilometers [1,806 kilometers is the actual range], and a high accuracy, could inflict strikes upon the Soviet Union's installations at which they are aimed in just 5 or 6 minutes after their launch. This would substantially alter the strategic situation.[4]

Nevertheless, Soviet INFs in Europe are strategic from the West European point of view. The Soviet understanding of the threat posed by the deployment of the U.S. INFs virtually ignores the security interests of the West European nations. According to Moscow's point of view, the "correlation of forces" between the United States and the Soviet Union at the nuclear level is what matters. No additional capacity of U.S. nuclear deterrence to protect the NATO European countries is deemed legitimate by the Soviets. Thus, it is reasonable from the Soviet point of view for Western Europe to be exposed to the vastly superior Eurostrategic weapons of the USSR. This clearly seems the point of view developed in the Soviet tract *The Threat to Europe* to explain to Western audiences the nature of the SS-20 "nonthreat" to West European security interests.

...Soviet military doctrine does not allow for a first or pre-emptive strike by the USSR. Even if we suppose that the Soviet Union is priming for a first strike (the "assumption" is completely false, though Western propaganda takes it for granted), it ought to be quite clear that in the present conditions any pre-emptive nuclear strike is senseless unless it destroys or at least substantially weakens the strategic nuclear potential of the other side's retaliatory capability. This the Soviet medium-range missiles cannot accomplish, because they do not reach as far as the United States and cannot hit U.S. intercontinental ballistic missiles. In the circumstances, a first strike in Western Europe would have no sense from any point of view, for it would only expose our country to riposte by an absolutely intact U.S. strategic arsenal.[5]

This position totally ignores the advantages such a first strike potentially gives the Soviets vis-a-vis the West European nuclear powers. The British and French, unlike the Soviets, certainly would characterize such a Soviet strike as strategic.

In light of the differing strategic assessments by the Soviets and the Americans of the theater nuclear balance, it is not surprising that the INF talks begun on 30 November 1981 showed little progress. Until March 1983, the basic American position was the "zero/zero" option. Under this proposal, the United States offered to cancel the planned deployment of the GLCMs and Pershing IIs if the Soviet Union would eliminate its SS-20s and SS-4s. The United States also asked for global limits on the INF systems to prevent the Soviets from redeploying these systems to Asia. Finally, the United States rejected any inclusion of British and French nuclear forces on the grounds that the U.S.-Soviet talks were bilateral and that British and French forces were not under U.S. control.

The Soviets totally rejected the zero/zero option and offered more limited proposals. One proposal was to restrict the number of SS-20s located west of the Urals to 300. In December 1982 the new leader of the Soviet Union, Iuri Andropov, offered to reduce Soviet SS-20s to a level equal to the strategic arsenals of Britain and France. Andropov's proposal would not require the Soviets to reduce or even limit the number of SS-20s in the Far East.

On 31 March 1983, President Reagan proposed an "interim solution" in which both sides would reduce, but not eliminate, their INF missiles. The United States would deploy a number short of the planned 572, and the Soviets would reduce to the same limit. The President mentioned no specific ceiling, but continued to insist on global limits on Soviet missiles and on excluding French and British systems.

The Soviets publicly rejected the Reagan initiative. On 2 April 1983, Andrei Gromyko, the Soviet Foreign Minister, declared: "If the position of the United States remains as now, as it has been stated, then there are no chances for agreement." Gromyko specifically rejected the global limits on Soviet missiles, for he indicated that the Soviets would want to withdraw some of the missiles from the European theater to Asia and "install them on sites from which they could not reach Western Europe. This is our business and our right." Gromyko stated that British and French nuclear missiles were an integral part of NATO and that "it is impossible to close our eyes to them." He said it would be an "absurdity" to ignore them in the total account. He also insisted that U.S. carrier-based aircraft be included in any agreement.[6]

In August, Andropov modified the Soviet stance in the INF negotiations. He stated in an interview in *Pravda*, and repeated in personal letters to West European leaders, that the Soviet Union would "liquidate" any Soviet medium-range nuclear missiles on its European territory that exceeded the level of French and British nuclear forces if the United States would drop its plans to deploy 572 Pershing IIs and cruise missiles. The new twist was the use of the word "liquidate," which seemed to indicate that the Soviet Union would not merely relocate these missiles elsewhere on its territory.[7]

President Reagan responded to Andropov's initiative with a proposal of his own. Reagan's proposal, announced before the UN

General Assembly, indicated a willingness to lower the number of U.S. systems to be deployed, especially the Pershing IIs, and to ease the total allowance of SS-20s in the Soviet arsenal.[8]

Andropov quickly denounced Reagan's proposals in very harsh terms. In a formal statement issued by the Soviet government in late September, the Soviet leader argued the following:

> ...the essence of the so-called new move by the United States, which is being advertised as munificent, again comes down to a proposal to have the two sides agree on the number of Soviet medium-range missiles to be dismantled and on the number of American missiles to be deployed in Europe in addition to the nuclear potential already possessed by NATO.[9]

Just before the initial deployments of the new U.S. systems in mid-November, the Reagan administration made another offer to the Soviets. The key element of the new proposal was to establish a "global" limitation of 420 nuclear warheads for each side on medium-range missiles deployed in Europe and Asia.[10] This limit would allow the Soviets to have 140 SS-20s but would legitimize an equal number of American systems. The Soviets rejected this proposal too because their basic position was that no new American missiles should be permitted in Europe.[11]

In short, the two sides remained far apart throughout the negotiations in 1983. The difficulty in concluding an agreement has been rooted in the different interests of the two sides. The Soviets' European INF systems provide them with a "nuclear firebreak" that makes the European conventional warfighting option more credible. These systems also provide the Soviets with nuclear options short of an all-out exchange with the United States. Politically, the conflict within the West over the U.S. missile deployment serves Soviet interests in exacerbating strains in West-West relations. These tensions may have already reduced one major concern of the Soviets, namely, that the limited deployment decision of December 1979 might simply be the beginning of more significant U.S. INF deployments in Europe. Also, the Soviets hope to abort French and British nuclear modernization in order to reduce the threat to themselves. French and British nuclear forces complicate the Soviet warfighting strategy in Europe and form the core of a potential European nuclear force.

For the Americans, deploying INF systems in Europe enhances the credibility of the flexible response strategy by more effectively coupling U.S. systems with European forces. By enhancing the credibility of flexible response, the United States is able to strengthen its political relations with Western Europe and to reduce Soviet influence.

Thus, it was not surprising when the Soviets walked away from the negotiating table in Geneva in late November 1983. But even though the interests of the two sides are deeply divergent, it is conceivable that some agreement can be reached in the future. As the Alliance deploys its new missiles, the Soviets might become convinced that it is militarily in their interest to have as low a level of deployment as possible. But outside this possibility, the chances for an agreement seem slight.

The French Reaction

Even before NATO's decision, the French had been sensitive to the problems of any European theater nuclear arms talks. Throughout the 1970s, many French analysts expressed concern about the political and military impact on Western Europe of the U.S.-Soviet SALT I and II treaties. On the one hand, the American concept of strategic parity seemed to underscore balances in intercontinental systems and to deemphasize the significance of American nuclear weapons for the defense of Europe. Thus, there was concern that the Americans were "decoupling" American nuclear weapons from the defense of the European theater. On the other hand, the Soviets' effort to have strategic parity equated with their concept of "equal security" was also worrisome. The Soviets were seen as desiring throughout the arms control negotiations of the 1970s to have Soviet "strategic" nuclear systems weighed against French and British nuclear systems, as well as U.S. intercontinental and "forward-based" systems (those U.S. nuclear systems deployed in Europe and theoretically capable of striking Soviet territory). The Soviets were thereby striving for nuclear superiority in the guise of a quest for equal security.

Representative of the French point of view is Jean-Marie Guehenno's analysis of the U.S.-Soviet SALT negotiations in the 1970s. Guehenno is currently the cultural attache at the French consulate general in New York, but at the time the article was written, he was deputy director of the planning staff at the French foreign ministry. According to Guehenno, the central contradiction of the SALT II treaty is that it emphasizes parity yet "accepts a definition of strategic weapons that is utterly asymmetrical from a European perspective."[12] Any Soviet nuclear weapons capable of striking West European territory must be considered strategic from the West European point of view. But it was not clear to Guehenno that the Americans understood this.

When the Americans acknowledged that they had reached essential equivalence with the Soviets, it could only have two interpretations, from a Soviet viewpoint. It meant a balance in Europe that was not included in the agreement but would be formalized in a future negotiation (SALT III). Or it meant there was no balance, no equivalence in Europe, but this imbalance did not jeopardize the essential equivalence between the two superpowers, either because Europe was not important from a strategic point of view or because a TNF [theater nuclear force] imbalance in Europe could be considered as a marginal problem provided there was a strategic balance at the central level.[13]

In addition to raising the general problem of how the Soviets might try to exploit contradictions in Western policy, Guehenno was concerned lest the Soviets be able to legitimize their claim to include French nuclear weapons as part of the "equivalent" Western nuclear potential against which the Soviets could weigh their forces. If there were a negotiated balance in European theater nuclear weapons with all Western forces counted, then any new deployments of French nuclear systems would come at the expense of Western strategic systems taken as a whole. The result would be to increase conflict within the West over nuclear weapon deployments, to Soviet advantage.

Once a common ceiling implicitly including French forces has been established, even if there is no French participation, the implicit relation between French deployments and subsequent American dismantlements or Soviet additional deployments will antagonize the French and the Americans, and more dangerously, the French and the West Germans. The French nuclear contribution to European security will appear as an exclusive alternative to the American guarantee and will confront the Germans with an impossible choice between the French nuclear deterrent and the American umbrella. Any additional French deployment might be perceived as having a decoupling effect in the alliance.[14]

The concerns expressed by Guehenno have been widely shared throughout the French government in the 1970s and 1980s and have shaped French responses to the Euromissile crisis. The period in which the initial deployment decision was debated, however, spanned the administrations of two French Presidents, each of whom has handled the issue in a different manner.

The administration of President Giscard d'Estaing supported the U.S. deployment of Euromissiles but, as Raymond Aron noted, "was wary of stating so publicly."[15] The Giscard administration argued that it was not necessary for France to come out in public support of the double decision. France was neither a member of the integrated military command nor a prospective recipient of the new American missiles. Jean Klein characterized the administration's policy in these terms:

Giscard d'Estaing considered that a decision to improve the strategy of flexible response did not concern France directly and thus that it would be misleading for France to approve a modernization with which it could not be associated. Besides, the 14 NATO countries had proposed to negotiate on the limitation of nuclear weapons in the framework of SALT, and there were good reasons to fear that the French nuclear deterrent would be included in this process. Because in the past the Soviet Union had looked on French and British forces as forward-based systems, their fate would inevitably be discussed during the negotiations. Nevertheless, Giscard d'Estaing, aware of the need for NATO to keep the balance, did not oppose measures to improve the military posture of the West.[16]

Giscard d'Estaing would later claim that he had planned to announce a "parallel" action with the American deployments in 1983. France would announce its plan to deploy a new missile, either a mobile IRBM or cruise missile, in response to the SS-20 threat.[17] Associates of Giscard have continued to assert during his successor's term that France's private support of the Euromissile deployment was preferable to overt, public support because public support inevitably induced the Soviets to demand compensation for French missiles in the INF forum.[18] Former West German Chancellor Schmidt also supported this contention.[19]

Giscard d'Estaing's rival for the Presidency, François Mitterrand, began a public campaign to denounce the Soviet SS-20 deployments and the threat they posed. Shortly after the NATO double decision was taken he stated: "It seems to me that the United States has been able to preserve a worldwide [military] superiority, but in Europe, Soviet superiority is established."[20] He also became increasingly critical of President Giscard d'Estaing's unwillingness to deal openly with the threat posed by Soviet Euromissiles.[21]

Mitterrand as President went one step further shortly after his election. In June 1981, during the first visit of Chancellor Schmidt, Mitterrand publicly endorsed the NATO decision. Mitterrand went further in an interview with *Der Stern* and indicated that deployment should precede negotiations, given the Eurostrategic imbalances.[22]

Throughout the Euromissile crisis, Mitterrand's administration frequently and vociferously supported the U.S. missile deployments. Most dramatically, President Mitterrand addressed the German Parliament on 20 January 1983 and expressed his direct support for the scheduled U.S. deployment of Euromissiles later that year.

"Whoever would bet on the decoupling of the European continent and the American continent would put into question the maintenance of equilibrium and thus the maintenance of peace," Mitterrand warned his West German audience. "I think, and I say it, that this decoupling is in itself dangerous, and I hope ardently that the Geneva negotiations will help to avert a danger that weighs particularly on the European partners that do not have nuclear weapons."[23]

Nonetheless, the support that the Mitterrand administration gave the double decision was tinged by sentiments within his political party, the Parti Socialiste Français (PSF). There was a desire within the PSF to restore the Eurostrategic balance, not to reestablish American nuclear superiority. As Jacques Huntzinger, the PSF's director for international relations, argued: "At the time when François Mitterrand was elected President, Europe was confronted with a situation of disequilibrium in favor of the Soviet Union, a disequilibrium that constituted the principal threat to peace. But we do not favor disequilibrium in favor of the Americans either, which will push us in dangerous directions also. This is why we have condemned Reagan's star wars program and why we question the rationale for the massive rearmament associated with American intercontinental nuclear arms."[24]

Mitterrand himself reflected such sentiments in his visit to Washington in March 1984. For Mitterrand, the Euromissile crisis was entering its third phase by early 1984. In the first phase, Moscow sought to gain political leverage over the Western Alliance by deploying its Euromissiles. In the second phase, the West resisted Soviet political "blackmail" and began to deploy its own Euromissiles. In the new, third phase, the West could reopen dialogue with Moscow, having demonstrated solidarity within the Alliance.[25] Dialogue with the East to establish "genuine" balance in East-West relations remains a deeply felt desire within the PSF.

The French government's involvement in the Euromissile issue deepened when Andropov proposed to reduce the Soviet SS-20 force to the level of British and French strategic nuclear warheads. The French government categorically rejected the inclusion of its nuclear systems in the INF talks. On the very day that Andropov's proposal for inclusion of French systems was made (21 December 1982), Foreign Minister Claude Cheysson characterized it as simply a means of "diverting the discussion."[26] On his first official visit to Moscow in February 1983, Cheysson emphasized to the Soviets that France would never agree to Andropov's proposal.[27] In discussions held in

June 1983 with members of the West European Union, Cheysson articulated the major reason for rejecting inclusion.

> The negotiations on intermediate-range nuclear forces must be carried out on a sound basis. Unfortunately, however, one of the two partners is trying to deflect the debate from its real objective in order to conceal the real problems more effectively. Attention is thus being focused on the third forces--French and British--when those forces have no place in these negotiations since their aim has never been to counter medium-range forces and since, in the strategy of deterrence of the strong by the weak, they are the means of deterring any enemy from using its full arsenal or even threatening to resort to it. In the face of the superpowers' excessive potential, these forces, as is known, guarantee and determine their holders' independence. France's nuclear forces will not be the subject of negotiations. That is out of the question....[28]

Prime Minister Pierre Mauroy in September 1983 elaborated on the government's position in an address before the Institute for Higher National Defense Studies (IHEDN).

> We do not intend to be involved, directly or indirectly, in the two Soviet-American negotiations in Geneva. Indeed the French nuclear deterrent forces have been limited to the minimum strictly necessary to ensure our deterrent's credibility. Our arsenal is therefore in no way comparable with those of the United States and the Soviet Union, which, for their part, have a nuclear overkill capacity. Moreover, the result of this is that there are many real possibilities for reducing the Soviet and American arsenals whereas France cannot drop below the threshold of credibility without casting doubt on its independence and security.[29]

The Soviet proposal to include the French systems created a diplomatic problem for the French. They had to persuade the non-nuclear NATO countries that the exclusion of French missiles from the INF talks was not a serious impediment to a U.S.-Soviet agreement. The French government had to counter the Soviet effort, in Pascal Boniface's words, to make France and Britain "responsible for an eventual failure [of the negotiations] at Geneva."[30]

Partially in response to external pressures, the French government did stake out its conditions for participating in some future arms limitation talks. President Mitterrand, in a speech delivered before the UN General Assembly on 28 September 1983, laid out three preconditions for French involvement in nuclear arms limitation talks among the five nuclear powers.[31] There would have to be a significant and verifiable reduction in the two superpowers' excessive levels of nuclear arms; there would have to be significant progress in conventional and chemical disarmament in Europe; and there could be no significant upgrading of antiballistic missile systems.[32]

In effect, the government was attempting to clarify the threat against which it was trying to protect France. The French forces were small and in no way comparable in kind to the superpowers'. As Prime Minister Mauroy put it, "In order for France to be able to envision participating in a global negotiation, it would be necessary for the two superpowers to have already decided to reduce their nuclear armaments in such a proportion that the gap between their potential and ours would be changed in kind."[33] The gap in strategic capability between France and the superpowers was just too great for France to pretend to negotiate in kind. Also, France faced a significant threat from the Soviet Union in terms of conventional forces and chemical weapons; France relies on its nuclear weapons to deter the Soviets from using military force of any kind, not just nuclear weapons. Finally, the French are very concerned about the ballistic missile defense (BMD) race between the superpowers. France needs more warheads to ensure an ability to penetrate current or future Soviet BMD systems. No controls on French offensive weapons are even thinkable in an atmosphere of intense superpower BMD competition.

While maintaining a vigorous diplomatic effort abroad, the Mitterrand administration faced a challenge at home from its junior partner in the governing coalition, the Parti Communiste Français (PCF).[34] During the course of the Euromissile crisis in 1983, the PCF progressively disassociated itself from Mitterrand's INF policy. The PCF opposed the language of the 5-year military program law that identified the Soviet Union as the major military threat to France. The deputies of the PCF in the national assembly abstained from voting for the section of the law in which this language appeared. For example, one PCF deputy argued that "designating a single potential adversary is an error, the gravity of which is apparent when one observes American military interventions in Central America and the Middle East."[35]

The next major step by the PCF was to attack Mitterrand's actions at the Williamsburg summit of the industrialized nations held in May 1983. At this summit, Mitterrand signed a joint declaration with the other Western leaders in which the security of their countries was described as "indivisible," despite France's special position in the Alliance.[36] The PCF's leaders chose to seize on this occasion to argue for including France in the INF talks. Their argument was that France had given up its neutrality in the Euromissile issue. In supporting NATO's INF deployment and declaring that its security was indivisible from that of the other Western powers, France had served notice that its strategic weapons were an integral component of the Alliance's arsenal. Neutrality had been so compromised that France must participate in the INF talks.[37] To symbolize the distance between the PSF and PCF, Georges Marchais, leader of the PCF, traveled to Moscow in July. Shortly after his trip, Marchais explained the PCF's position as follows:

> If we want to launch a nuclear disarmament process in Europe, it is necessary to start by making an accurate count of all the weapons of this type that exist on our continent, on both sides.
>
> Should the French nuclear deterrent force be considered within this framework? Or should we pretend it does not exist? The answer is straightforward: France is a member of the Atlantic Alliance, and, as such, is bound by the resulting obligations. Furthermore, the president of the Republic, by signing the Williamsburg declaration, agreed to define the Western countries' security as "indivisible" and "viewed on a comprehensive basis." How could anybody think it would be possible to simultaneously say to the Americans: "In case of misfortune, you can count on us," and to the Soviets: "You have no right to count us on one side or the other?"
>
> Observing that the French nuclear deterrent force has to be considered within the framework of this vital count is simply taking account of the existing situation. It is obvious that it is not satisfactory for the superpowers to discuss this situation alone, without France; that is precisely why, as I said, we are asking that our country be associated in the Geneva negotiations, with all other European countries.[38]

The PCF, however, stood alone within France on the Euromissile issue. There was strong sentiment in France to resist Soviet pressure, so much so that an article in *Le Monde* published shortly after U.S. missile deployments began in November was entitled, "A Consensus From Which the PCF Has Excluded Itself."[39]

The French reaction to the Euromissile crisis, especially as embodied in the policy of the Mitterrand administration, has been shaped by several factors. Significantly, the French have wished to protect their nuclear modernization program from being derailed by external or internal pressures. As Prime Minister Mauroy put it, "France cannot accept constraints on the modernization of its nuclear forces. It adheres strictly to the definition of a threshold of nuclear adequacy. The modernization effort that we have started is based on the urgent need, in the face of the development of the threat, to maintain our deterrent's credibility."[40] The French deeply resent the Soviet Union's attempts to gain diplomatic leverage on the French modernization effort through the INF talks or, as many French believe, domestically through the PCF.

In addition, the French, throughout the 1970s and 1980s, have been skeptical of the U.S.-Soviet arms control process.[41] With the single exception of the Antiballistic Missile Treaty, the French have been less than enthusiastic supporters of superpower arms control talks. The French see these talks as part of the East-West political struggle. They are not a realm where technocrats make decisions to constrain technological modernizations. As John Vinocur has noted, "For the French, the central defense tasks of the next two decades are essentially political. At the highest level, these missions are seen as maintaining the American presence in Europe...."[42] They do not want the Soviets to be able to use arms control talks to divide Europe from America, although they see exactly this as a prime Soviet objective.

The reinforcement of American ties to European defense has been a central French concern in the Euromissile crisis. French analysts frequently express doubts about the political will of Americans to use nuclear weapons and have seen the U.S. INF deployments as an American action tying America's fate more closely to that of Europe in the case of war in Europe.

Mitterrand has viewed the strengthening of the "coupling" of European and American defense as a critical means, paradoxically, for Western Europe to become more independent. François Gorand has expressed this paradox as follows:

> The question of the Euromissiles only reveals an essential mutation that many others have described, which one can sum up in these simple words: the end, once and for all, of American military superiority over the Soviet Union on the central level and in Europe. This "hardening" of the political-strategic context results in an exacerbation of the ambiguities of the Western defense system that De Gaulle--always De Gaulle--already revealed in the 1960s. These ambiguities were tolerable in the Western world that was more confident of itself in the 1960s, but increasingly less so in a world that is more dangerous. The response to this change must be a consolidation of the "coupling" by the Pershing IIs, but cannot be limited to that. Even if the Soviet Union fails in its aim this time, there is every possibility that its strategy, which simply consists of creating the conditions for maximum intensification of differences in interest between the United States and Europe, will one day or another succeed if Europe should continue to depend on the American commitment for its security to the extent it now does. Furthermore, the Germans' awareness of these ambiguities, combined with the rediscovery of their "Germanness," requires, if we do not want the FRG to fall back on the neutralist option, that something other than the NATO option be offered to it.
>
> In other words, the recoupling by the Pershing missiles cannot be an end in itself, but only a necessary condition for control of Europe's destiny by Europeans. It is up to France to defend the Euromissiles, not in the name of keeping NATO static, but based on a vision of the future of Europe as Mitterrand told the

Bundestag, emphasizing that there can be no true dialogue with the East without a balance of forces.[43]

In his comment Gorand raised another of the critical factors affecting the French position. The French have been very troubled by what they perceive to be the deteriorating situation on defense issues in a number of West European countries, notably those infected with "pacifism." During the intense debate on INFs, a flurry of books and articles appeared that emphasized the threat pacifism poses to Europe.[44]

Special concern has been expressed within the French elite about the future of Germany. There is a long-standing distrust of West Germany's detente policy, and in particular, concern about the "Rapallo spirit," whereby the FRG might strike a deal with the Soviets to exchange reunification for neutralization. In addition, the French have questioned the reliability of the Social Democratic Party (SPD) opposition to the Kohl government. The SPD is frequently characterized as in the throes of a debilitating debate on security policy, the effect of which is to undercut West German will to resist Soviet pressure in future political crises. The French see their position on the Euromissile issue as lending support to those forces resisting pacifism in Europe and in the FRG in particular. President Mitterrand's speech in the Bundestag was a reflection of this French concern.

Finally, the French are concerned with countering what they perceive to be the negative aspects of Soviet diplomacy toward Western Europe.[45] From the French point of view, the Soviets tried to use the Euromissile crisis to divide the Americans from the Europeans and to obstruct the development of greater security cooperation among the Europeans by portraying the French and British nuclear modernizations as disruptive elements in East-West relations.

From the French point of view, a number of lessons have been learned and critical challenges identified in the course of the Euromissile crisis. First, the Soviet Union appears more than willing to attempt to use its military power to blackmail Western Europe. The Mitterrand administration's view of this problem is evident in the following comment made by Foreign Minister Cheysson in 1983:

I am talking of "peaceful development" and not just "peace" because I would not want people to think that the French government believes in the possibility of a war triggered by the Soviets. On the contrary, we are convinced of the obsessive fear of war that exists in the USSR. My visit to that country gave me a physical perception of this; because I went to Leningrad, which is the very illustration of the profound reasons why the Soviets hate war. But there is no contradiction between hating war and wanting to have an instrument of power at one's disposal that would allow one sometimes to put pressure on certain parties in the other camp.[46]

Second, in spite of France's policy of independence in security matters, a firm alliance with the Americans is seen as necessary to counter the Soviets. According to Cheysson,

despite major changes on the international scene over the past 34 years, none of the reasons that made the Atlantic Alliance necessary has lost its value.... As then, the European countries cannot by themselves secure the defense of their "space." As then, the presence in close proximity of powerful Warsaw Pact armies and the Soviet nuclear forces gives rise to a link of security across the Atlantic.

This link implies that any idea of aggression against the European countries should be made impossible and senseless through the prospect of response by American nuclear weapons.... The Soviet Union deployed the SS-20's with the express purpose of dividing and compartmentalizing the rationale of deterrence. These arms cannot reach the heart of the alliance, the U.S., yet have the capacity to destroy in the space of a few moments all the means of retaliation of Europe itself.... In political terms this means that an attempt is being made to undo the trans-Atlantic link and to separate the defense of Europe from that of the U.S. The aim is to decouple the ultimate means of deterrence from those of the defense of the "European glacis."

Thus doubt as to the credibility of American deterrence is surreptitiously creeping into the picture. In some quarters in Europe--fewer than they are said to be--there is a vague and growing feeling that American protection is uncertain and that uncertain protection is more dangerous than no protection at all. So Europeans are coming to feel more frightened of the arms you [the Americans] are sending to Europe to protect them than of the arms build-up in the East.

This malaise is difficult to understand in the U.S. It is wrongly perceived as a sign of relinquishment, of giving up, and many Americans are being tempted by the idea of pulling back. Reacting this way would consummate the very thing that must be avoided. The remedy therefore lies in greater deterrence backed by American strength and in dispelling all doubt regarding it.[47]

Third, a policy of independence or, more accurately, of a country's responsibility for its own defense, is perceived by the French to be critical to that country's ability to reject pacifism or Soviet pressures to become "neutralized." As *Le Monde* noted, "It is not just a coincidence that France is today the European country least affected by neutralism and pacifism while Holland, once ultra-Atlanticist, is the ally that most seeks to escape its responsibilities for Euromissiles."[48]

Fourth, the Soviets are attempting to isolate nuclear weapons as the major threat to peace. According to French Defense Minister Charles Hernu, the Soviets seek the "complete denuclearization of

Western Europe." Hernu, however, insists that nuclear weapons are the only reliable means of preventing war in Europe.

> Nuclear deterrence has been the best means of preventing conflicts for more than 30 years and it still is.... In addition, we in Europe know that any war, be it conventional, chemical or nuclear, would be a holocaust. We are also afraid that any conflict, even a so-called "conventional" one, even one accompanied by the "no first use" pledge, might inevitably degenerate into a nuclear conflict. Thus, our aim is to prevent war. And only nuclear deterrence is capable of doing that.[49]

The lessons learned lead to the conclusion that Western Europe needs to develop a more independent system of defense in which political responsibility curbs the pacifist "temptation." Greater independence must not come at the expense of a continued alliance with the U.S., for American forces, especially nuclear ones, remain the critical counterbalance to the Soviet threat to Europe. Nuclear weapons, especially West European ones, are an important component in Western Europe's ability to be independent yet bind the Americans to Europe.

Comparing the Soviet and French Positions

The Soviets' own Eurostrategic systems provide them with a "nuclear firebreak" that makes their European conventional warfighting option more credible and with nuclear options short of an all-out exchange with the United States. Politically, the conflict within the West over the U.S. missile deployment serves Soviet interests in exacerbating tensions in West-West relations. Also, the Soviets hope to forestall French and British nuclear modernization in order to reduce the nuclear threat to themselves.

For the French, the necessity for Western Eurostrategic modernization has both military and political underpinnings. Militarily, the French want the West (United States, Britain, and France) to enhance its nuclear capability in Europe, thereby under-cutting the Soviets' conventional and nuclear warfighting options. The French believe that a credible nuclear response to Soviet aggression in Europe, conventional or nuclear, is still the most reliable means of defense. Politically, the French see the U.S. Euromissile deployment as a means for coupling European with American defense. The French also wish to provide themselves with diplomatic breathing room so they can modernize their nuclear forces and perhaps define a broader European role for their security policy in an atmosphere that is free from external pressures.

The Soviet position conflicts with the French position on several points. The Soviets hope to enhance the flexibility of their military options; the French wish to reduce Soviet flexibility. The Soviets wish to decouple U.S. nuclear forces from European defense; the French hope to see coupling enhanced. The Soviets want to isolate the French diplomatically in Europe in order to abort the development of a broader European role for French security policy; the French hope to protect themselves from such Soviet pressure. The Soviets hope to delegitimize nuclear weapons as a reliable means for Western defense; the French hope to relegitimize this role for nuclear weapons. The Soviets wish to promote the reduction of West European defense cooperation; the French wish to enhance cooperation.

Conflicting positions reflect diverging interests. The French want to enhance the Europeanization of the Western Alliance. French independence, it is hoped, will stimulate Europe to play a greater role in its own defense while remaining firmly anchored in the Western Alliance. The Soviets consider such Europeanization of the Alliance to be virtually a worst-case scenario, in which Western Europe is able to better fend for itself in security matters and the Americans remain firm allies able to operate more effectively outside Europe. A major motivation of Soviet diplomatic activity in the Euromissile crisis has been precisely to forestall any such emergence of their worst-case scenario.

In short, the military and political roles of Soviet nuclear weapons in Europe and of French nuclear weapons are in direct conflict. We now turn to a further elaboration of these roles.

Notes

1. V. Kulikov, "Interview on Warsaw Pact," *Neues Deutschland*, 14 May 1981, translated in *Foreign Broadcast Information Service* [hereinafter *FBIS*] *Daily Report: Soviet Union*, 20 May 1981, BB-2.

2. B. Ponomarev, "The Most Urgent Task of Our Time," *Le Monde*, 23 December 1980, translated in *FBIS Daily Report: Soviet Union*, 24 December 1980, AA-2.

3. L. Brezhnev, "Talks with the Swedish Social Democratic Party Chairman in Moscow," *Tass*, 12 June 1981.

4. D. Ustinov in Pravda, 24 July 1981, translated in *FBIS Daily Report: Soviet Union*, 27 July 1981, AA-2.

5. *The Threat to Europe* (Moscow: Progress, 1981), 20.

6. *New York Times*, 3 April 1983.

7. *New York Times*, 27 August 1983.

8. *Washington Post*, 27 September 1983.

9. *New York Times*, 29 September 1983.

10. *Washington Post*, 14 November 1983.

11. *Washington Post*, 18 December 1983.

12. This paper was written in 1979 but only published in 1983. Jean Marie Guehenno, "Strategic Versus European Arms Negotiations: The Limits of Complementarity," in *The Western Panacea: Constraining Soviet Power Through Negotiation*, ed. Uwe Nerlich (Cambridge, Mass.: Ballinger Publishing Co., 1983), 364.

13. Ibid., 363.

14. Ibid., 364-365.

15. Raymond Aron in *L'Express*, 15-21 April 1983, 91.

16. Jean Klein, "Current Aspects of Security and Arms Control in Europe," unpublished paper, 14-15.

17. *Le Monde*, 19 February 1983.

18. See, for example, the argument by Gabriel Robin in *Le Monde*, 12 March 1983.

19. *Le Monde*, 23 June 1983.

20. As quoted by Michael M. Harrison, "Mitterrand's France in the Atlantic System," *Political Science Quarterly* 99 (Summer 1984): 228.

21. *Le Monde*, 3 July 1980.

22. *Le Monde*, 9 July 1981.

23. See speech released by Présidence de la République, Service de Presse, 20 January 1983, 4.

24. Jacques Huntzinger, "La France et les superpuissances," *Politique d'aujourd'hui*, November 1983, 62.

25. *Le Monde*, 24 March 1984.

26. *Le Monde*, 23 December 1982.

27. *Le Monde*, 17-19 February 1983.

28. *Le Monde*, 9 June 1983.

29. Pierre Mauroy, "La Stratégie de la France," *Défense nationale*, November 1983, 10.

30. Pascal Boniface, "Genève: La logique de l'échec," *Défense nationale*, April 1984, 55.

31. See speech released by Présidence de la République, Service de Presse, 28 September 1983.

32. For a further elaboration of the French position, see Pascal Boniface, "Paris-Genève--les étapes nécessaires," *La Lettre de l'INSED*, November 1983, 3.

33. Pierre Mauroy, "Vers un nouveau modèle d'armée," *Défense nationale*, November 1982, 23.

34. See, for example, N. Gnesotto, "Le PCF et les euromissiles," *Politique étrangère*, 1983, no. 3:701-712.

35. *Le Matin*, 12 May 1983.

36. *Le Monde*, 31 May 1983.

37. *Le Monde*, 2 June 1983.

38. *L'Humanité*, 20 July 1983.

39. *Le Monde*, 21 November 1983.

40. Mauroy, "La Stratégie de la France," 11.

41. For a recent pessimistic appraisal by a French official of the future of U.S.-Soviet arms control, see Philippe Boone, "L'Affaire des FNI et l'avenir des négociations stratégiques," *Défense nationale*, May 1984, 33-44.

42. *New York Times*, 8 June 1983.

43. Francois Gorand, "France et les euromissiles," *Commentaire*, Fall 1983, 549.

44. See, for example, Pierre Lellouche, ed., *Pacifisme et dissuasion* (Paris: Economica Press, 1983).

45. See, for example, Michel Tatu, *La Bataille des euromissiles* (Paris: Editions du Seuil, 1983). Also, see the discussion throughout the section on the Euromissile crisis in *Défense nationale,* August-September 1983, 5-62.

46. See the interview with Claude Cheysson, "Diplomatie: l'empreinte française," *Politique internationale,* Summer 1983, 14.

47. *Wall Street Journal,* 25 February 1983.

48. As quoted in the *Washington Post,* 10 June 1983.

49. *Le Monde,* 2 December 1982.

2
Soviet Nuclear Weapons in Europe

This chapter describes and analyzes the military and political roles of Soviet nuclear weapons in Europe. Paradoxically, the deployment of new-generation Soviet nuclear weapons strengthens the ability of the Soviets to conduct conventional military operations in Europe. By deploying new nuclear systems more capable of surviving an extended period of conventional warfare, the Soviets can more confidently prepare to wage an all-conventional campaign. The new Western Eurostrategic systems are an important threat to the viability of the Soviets' all-conventional option and complicate their attempt to exercise escalation dominance. The Soviets had hoped to reduce the Western threat by political bluster and arms diplomacy.

Politically, the superiority of Soviet theater nuclear systems (in the context of U.S.-Soviet parity in intercontinental nuclear systems) has been useful in increasing political tensions in the Western Alliance. The Soviets have sought simultaneously to decouple Western Europe from the U.S. and to discourage West European military integration, especially the development of West European nuclear capabilities. The deployment of the new Western Eurostrategic systems tends to undercut these twin Soviet goals. Coupling will be increased and French and British nuclear capability enhanced as modernization proceeds.

The Military Role of Soviet Nuclear Weapons in Europe

The basis for the exercise of political influence by the Soviet Union in Western Europe has been its military power. As R. A. Mason has noted, "...since 1945 the Soviet Union has been in no position to exert economic pressure and any spread of Marxist-Leninist ideology has taken place despite its example rather than in its emulation. Apart from perennial encouragement of internal divisive and disruptive elements it is self-evident that military strength has been a primary instrument of Soviet diplomacy toward Western Europe."[1]

The political role of nuclear weapons in the Soviet exercise of influence is conditioned by perceptions of their military role. Hence, before analyzing the political role of Soviet nuclear weapons, it is necessary to identify how they might be used in a military confrontation in Europe.

As a European power, the Soviet Union would hope to fight a war against the West in such a way as to limit damage to the European landmass. The Soviets would like to be able to destroy Western forces in Europe to the extent necessary to ensure the capture of Europe, but without excessive damage to the Soviet Union, primarily, and Europe, secondarily.

The Soviets expect a war in Europe to involve substantial conventional operations.[2] Their key goal during conventional operations would be to degrade Western military forces in Europe, especially nuclear forces. The Soviets have become increasingly sensitive to the possibility and even the desirability of withholding nuclear strikes as long as possible or, in other words, of prolonging conventional operations in a war with the West as long as it is feasible to do so. As *Strategic Survey* has commented, "...the presumed role of Soviet theater nuclear forces (TNF) would be to deter NATO from nuclear use while its nuclear capabilities were being degraded by Soviet conventional forces. Soviet TNF would thus be used for the preemption mission only when positive warning had been received that a strike by NATO's residual nuclear forces was imminent."[3] Thus, a key military objective of Soviet nuclear weapons in Europe is to make a conventional warfighting option more viable.

The Soviets deploy three basic types of nuclear weapon systems for potential use in a European nuclear war: short-, medium-, and long-range theater nuclear weapons. Soviet short-range, or battlefield, nuclear weapons are designed for use in relative proximity to Warsaw Pact forces. Soviet battlefield nuclear weapons consist of artillery pieces (especially 152-mm guns, both the self-propelled and towed versions) and short-range missile systems (the truck-mounted Frog and its replacement, the SS-21). Although NATO has a numerical advantage in battlefield nuclear weapons, the Warsaw Pact has significantly more short-range missile launchers. And as one authoritative Western source notes, "...the greater range, and consequently the improved target coverage and survivability, of the

Warsaw Pact's land-based missiles more than compensates for NATO's numerical advantage."[4]

Soviet medium-range theater nuclear systems consist of tactical aircraft that can carry conventional or nuclear armament and medium-range missile systems, the Scud B and the SS-12 Scaleboard (and their successors, the SS-23 and SS-22 respectively). The SS-22 and SS-23 have greater survivability, improved maneuver capabilities, and better reliability. These improved systems enhance the Soviets' conventional warfighting capabilities. As Stephen Meyer has noted, "These missiles might be called upon to survive an extended period of conventional warfare, throughout which enemy reconnaissance would try to locate them in preparation for attacks against them."[5]

The Soviets have steadily improved their capabilities to deliver nuclear strikes with their medium-range forces. This trend has been especially evident with regard to the enhancement over the past decade of the nuclear ground-attack capabilities of Soviet tactical aircraft. The most capable Soviet tactical aircraft, the Fencer and Flogger, were introduced in the mid-1970s and began to be deployed in significant numbers only in the late 1970s and early 1980s.

The Su-24 Fencer is the first modern Soviet aircraft specifically designed for ground attack. The Fencers have decisively strengthened the striking power of the Soviet air forces aimed at Western Europe. The Fencer can carry a large and diverse payload, including nuclear ordnance. It has the range to strike most significant military targets in Western Europe.

Although deployment of the Flogger did not begin until 1971, it is now the most widely deployed aircraft in Soviet Frontal Aviation. The Flogger D/J, or MiG-27, is a nuclear-capable, ground-attack aircraft that can attain high subsonic speed at low altitude.

Soviet long-range theater nuclear systems consist of a medium-range bomber force and an intermediate-range ballistic missile (IRBM) force. The medium-range bomber force consists of the Badger, Blinder and Backfire aircraft. The Badger (2,800-kilometer range) and the Blinder (3,100-kilometer range) are older systems, but they are being upgraded to extend their service life. These older aircraft will eventually be replaced by the new Backfire bomber, first deployed in 1974. The range of the Backfire, at 4,200 kilometers, is significantly greater than that of the Badger or Blinder. According to *Strategic Survey*, "This range allows it [the Backfire] to cover all of NATO Europe, as well as large areas of adjacent oceans, from bases in the USSR; perhaps equally important, it gives the aircraft increased loiter time at shorter range, and thus an enhanced capability to seek out mobile targets."[6]

The Soviet IRBM force consists of the older SS-4 and the new SS-20 medium-range missiles. The SS-4 missile uses liquid fuel and carries a single warhead. It is based in fixed silos and is potentially vulnerable to a preemptive NATO strike. The new SS-20 represents a significant improvement in every dimension. The SS-20 uses solid fuel, which allows it to be launched more quickly. The SS-20 is mobile, which makes it more capable of surviving preemptive strikes, and it carries three warheads, which significantly expands the target coverage of Soviet IRBMs. It is also much more accurate than the SS-4, giving it greater military utility.

The greater survivability of the SS-20 and the Soviets' ability to withhold Fencers and Backfires on their own territory allow the Soviets to ride out lengthy conventional operations more effectively and also provide them with improved nuclear warfighting capabilities. As Gregory Treverton has argued:

> The record of the last two decades clearly suggests that the USSR accords high priority to targeting Western Europe, probably a higher priority than most in the West have believed. The SS-20 underscores that priority. It demonstrates a traditional objective of Soviet efforts: to deter NATO's resort to nuclear weapons in war, to deter escalation if NATO goes nuclear and to have some chance of avoiding destruction on Soviet territory.[7]

If the Soviets thought in terms of conducting nuclear operations against NATO Europe, they would hope to draw a clear line between nuclear weapons used against European targets (East and West) and nuclear weapons used against Soviet or American territory. Several components in the Soviet theater nuclear arsenal would aid them in achieving this objective; others would not.

The short-range, or battlefield, nuclear weapons would provide the Soviets with a limited nuclear war option that would be compatible with limiting nuclear war to the European theater. Nuclear weapons would be limited in range, yield, and level of damage commensurate with the task of destroying NATO's military assets within Europe. From the standpoint of both warfighting and post-war recovery, limiting theater nuclear warfare to the level of battlefield weapons is desirable to the Soviets.

Use of either the medium- or long-range theater nuclear systems would involve serious possibilities of provoking at least selected nuclear strikes against Soviet territory. Nonetheless, the Soviets might try to generate a Eurostrategic option from their medium- and long-range theater nuclear systems. Such an option would involve a massive strike against NATO's theater nuclear assets, airfields, port facilities, and other military targets.

A Soviet Eurostrategic option might employ nuclear weapons located in Eastern Europe, perhaps supplemented by some long-range theater systems. The Scud-B and SS-23 missiles are already integrated into Soviet forces in Eastern Europe. The SS-12 Scaleboard and SS-22 are deployed on Soviet territory in peacetime but would move to Eastern Europe in wartime. The Warsaw Pact's nuclear-capable tactical aircraft could all operate from East European air bases. These medium-range systems would probably be supported by air strikes by Backfire, Badger, and Blinder bombers, which are normally based in the Soviet Union. If the Soviets were concerned to preserve fully the distinction between European and superpower territory, these systems could be deployed forward to Eastern Europe to provide more firepower for a Eurostrategic effort. One authoritative source notes that, "...SS-20 missiles are readily transportable and could be relocated westward at short notice."[8]

Such a Soviet Eurostrategic strike would be massive and designed to reduce significantly NATO's ability to continue the European war effort. The Warsaw Pact ground forces would then attempt to move quickly to exploit the results of the theater nuclear strikes and to occupy Western Europe.

Above all, Soviet TNF systems are deployed to deter the West's use of nuclear weapons. The Soviets would hope to combine nuclear deterrence with the erosion of Western nuclear capability during the conventional campaign. As Stephen Meyer has articulated the role of TNFs in contemporary Soviet military strategy:

> Soviet nuclear forces are assigned the mission of deterring enemy TNF employment, while Soviet conventional forces go about the task of locating and destroying them. The main mission of reconnaissance and intelligence operations, then, is to locate enemy nuclear forces in the theatre. Soviet TNF will be husbanded in rear areas, safe from enemy conventional strikes, while Soviet *conventional* forces whittle down enemy TNF. Soviet expectations are that, as the war evolves, the theatre nuclear balance (i.e., the correlation of nuclear forces in the theatre) will move steadily in the direction of greater Soviet preponderance.[9]

Nonetheless, if widespread nuclear use in the theater became necessary, Soviet conventional forces are designed to operate under nuclear battlefield conditions (to the extent to which one can prepare for such an operation). As Jeffrey Record has noted:

> A significant feature of the Soviet tanks and armored fighting vehicles introduced into service during the past decade and a half is their incorporation of extensive CBR (chemical, biological and radiological) defensive systems that afford Soviet ground forces a far higher degree of survivability on a contaminated battlefield than even the latest vehicles fielded by NATO, most of which lack collective overpressure systems and adequate filtration devices.... That the Soviet aim has been to develop truly dual-purpose "conventional" forces--capable of operating in either a nuclear or non-nuclear environment--is also evident in an unparalleled regime of CBR warfare training and in a refusal to sacrifice investment in numbers to achieve qualitative improvements.[10]

In short, the Soviets would hope to deter NATO from using nuclear weapons by having a credible threat of retaliation. The Soviets would clearly wish to avoid exchanging intercontinental strategic nuclear strikes with the United States. They would hope that the strategic nuclear balance, which deters politically in peacetime, would deter the United States militarily in wartime from engaging in massive intercontinental strikes against Soviet territory. Eurostrategic weapons, especially the SS-20s, are useful militarily for deterring escalation to any nuclear level. They are, therefore, a significant component in the Soviets' effort to make a conventional warfighting option more viable.

In other words, the Soviets are hoping to raise the nuclear threshold to enhance their conventional military options in Europe. And by enhanced conventional military power, the Soviets hope to increase their leverage over Western Europe. As R. A. Mason has argued:

> Any reduction of dependence on nuclear weapons by NATO would replace one set of military problems by another and would pose complicated questions of defence appropriations to member nations. It might reduce the chances of the early use of nuclear weapons in a European conflict but would certainly facilitate the implementation of the Soviet Union's own military doctrine. It is probable, therefore, that the raising of the nuclear threshold, unless it were to be accompanied by Warsaw Pact conventional arms reduction, would strengthen the military element in Soviet policy toward Western Europe.[11]

The Political Role of Soviet Nuclear Weapons in Europe

Soviet European nuclear forces serve the political objective of exacerbating strains in U.S.-West European relations, besides contributing to any actual military effort. For the Soviets, achieving parity with the United States in intercontinental nuclear systems has helped undermine the American nuclear guarantee for Western

Europe. A. F. Gorelova and Iu. P. Davydov have noted with favor the recognition by West Europeans that "...after the loss by the U.S. of its 'nuclear superiority' in the context of 'nuclear parity' with the USSR, the reliability of the American security guarantee for Western Europe has declined."[12] The deployment of Soviet theater nuclear systems is designed in part to erode further the American security guarantee for Western Europe and thereby to weaken the political ties between Western Europe and the United States.

"Atlanticism," in the Soviet view, has allowed the United States to exercise considerable influence over political and economic developments within Western Europe. From the Soviet perspective, an Atlanticized Europe is one in which American definitions of Western security needs dominate Western Europe's security interests and political and economic relationships with the Soviet Union. Such an Atlanticized Europe was able to exist only under the specific conditions of absolute American predominance over Western Europe that existed in the late 1940s and early 1950s. As G. A. Vorontsov has noted, an Atlanticized Europe has rested upon "the military, economic, and financial power of the United States, which guaranteed a commanding position in its relations with Western Europe."[13]

This type of Atlanticism has been seriously undercut by the changing balance of power (or, in Soviet terminology, the "shift in the correlation of forces") between the United States and Western Europe. The growth of West European economic power has led to the emergence of the West European "power center" in the capitalist world, a power center that has exercised growing assertiveness and even independence from the United States.[14]

In the Soviet view, "three centers of imperialism" have emerged, rather than a cohesive Western camp whose unity is enforced by American dominance.[15] The "correlation of forces" in the imperialist camp has shifted away from the United States in favor of Western Europe and Japan. This redistribution of power has increased "interimperialist contradictions." As O. Bogdanov argued:

> With the change in the balance of strength between the chief centers of imperialism, the capitalist powers tended gradually to substitute "polycentrism" for "U.S.-centrism" in their economic and political lines. This involved abandoning the scheme of international economic relations resting on U.S. supremacy. U.S. economic and political overlordship clashed with the weakening of the U.S. position in the world capitalist economy. As a result, foreign economic relations tend increasingly to become an important area of interimperialist rivalry within the triangle of the U.S., the EEC, and Japan.[16]

The growing assertiveness of Western Europe limits the American ability to take unilateral actions to define Western interests. This limitation has, in turn, substantially undercut U.S. global flexibility. As Voronstov added:

> Western Europe has now consolidated its economic weight and political influence to the extent that the United States cannot engage in any major actions in the international arena without its assistance and support. It is sufficient to recall Washington's persistent and extremely active endeavor to involve the West Europeans in "sanctions" against the USSR, the policy of confrontation with Iran, the plan for the creation of rapid deployment forces, and so forth.[17]

With the growing diversification of power in the Western world, American policymakers are trying to exercise leadership on the military front as a means of preserving U.S. political and economic dominance in the West. As the late N. N. Inozemtsev noted, an important aspect of the contemporary situation is that "the changes running against the United States in the economic and political positions in the leading West European countries and Japan have been taking place in the context of tremendous U.S. military superiority."[18] In other words, the United States is reduced to drawing upon its military dominance to protect its deteriorating position of leadership in the West. From a Soviet standpoint, NATO as an organization plays a major role in protecting American power in Western Europe and in limiting West European independence from U.S. security interests. As V. S. Shein underscored:

> Although U.S. economic, political, and even ideological positions in relation to Western Europe have become much weaker, particularly as a result of the development of West European integration, and now with the decline of American hegemony in the Atlantic world, NATO...has turned out to be the only instrument for imposing Washington's will on the states of Western Europe.[19]

The key lever through which the United States can exercise influence over NATO Europe is its nuclear weapons. As one group of Soviet analysts noted, "At the contemporary stage of the scientific-technological revolution in military affairs, the actual military potential of a given state depends primarily upon its possession or non-possession of nuclear weapons and the level of development of its nuclear-missile systems."[20] Given the overwhelming predominance of American nuclear arms within NATO, the United States is able to exercise a preponderant influence over NATO.

Nonetheless, the centrality of American nuclear weapons to NATO defense underscores a central contradiction between Western Europe and the United States. As the same group of Soviet analysts emphasized:

> The strategical calculations of the two centers of power make a strikingly different assessment of the character of a potential military conflict. In its endeavor to avoid destruction of its own territory the U.S. is oriented toward a limitation of operations to the European theater of action in the event of an armed conflict in this region, at least in its early stages. The West European military conceptions proceed from the necessity to ensure the broad participation of the U.S. in the conflict from the very moment of its inception. This diametrical opposition of their interests is breeding a chain reaction of fears in Western Europe and disagreements with the U.S. on such questions as the stationing of American troops in Western Europe, the reliability of the U.S.'s nuclear guarantees, the role of NATO outside of its geographical bounds, the possible involvement of Western Europe in the military undertakings of American global politics....[21]

Soviet Eurostrategic capability contributes to precisely this contradiction of interests between Western Europe and the United States. Parity in intercontinental systems tends to deter the United States from using these systems to defend Western Europe and hence raises questions within Western Europe about the reliability of U.S. nuclear guarantees.

The modernization of Soviet Eurostrategic arms contributes to the Soviet's capability to conduct a nuclear war limited to Europe. But when the United States has tried to strengthen its European theater nuclear forces, the Soviets have stressed the dangerous quality of American "limited nuclear war" doctrines. They do this in part to exacerbate West-West tensions and to impede Western military development.

To the United States, the Soviets emphasize the impossibility of a Eurostrategic war's being contained without escalation to intercontinental systems.[22] With such a claim the Soviets hope to convince the United States to cease developing theater nuclear forces with which to implement NATO's flexible response strategy.

To the West Europeans, the Soviets emphasize that U.S. preparation for, or emphasis upon, a limited nuclear war shows a lack of genuine American concern for West European security.[23] The Soviets thereby wish to convey the message that the United States is an offshore power not sharing the same security problems as the Soviet and West European "continental" powers.[24]

By pressuring both the American and European components of the Alliance, the Soviets hope to obstruct the development of Western strategic power. The Soviets wish to slow the further development of a

Eurostrategic rung of the U.S. escalation ladder. Also, the Soviets wish to undercut the process of modernization of French and British nuclear forces.

Thus, the Eurostrategic problem is a deeply political one. The Soviets hope to increase their deterrent capability, to increase their leverage against Western Europe, and to obstruct Western strategic development by maintaining their Eurostrategic superiority in the context of intercontinental strategic parity. Colin Gray's characterization of the strategic arms race as being "about politics" could not be more aptly applied than to the political objectives served by Soviet Eurostrategic deployments.[25]

The Impact of the Western Alliance's Eurostrategic Modernization

The opposition of the Soviet Union to the Western Alliance's Eurostrategic modernization is rooted in the negative effects of that modernization on the military and political roles of Soviet INF systems.[26] Militarily, the Soviets are concerned that the American, French, and British modernizations may so complicate Soviet military strategy that Western superiority can appear to be reestablished. Politically, the Soviets are concerned with the strengthening of U.S. ties to a Western Europe that will possess an enhanced independent nuclear capability as British and French forces are modernized.

The deployment of the new U.S. INF systems provides the Americans with a much more survivable nuclear force. The survivability of the new systems casts doubt on the Soviets' ability to preempt conventionally against them. The range and accuracy of the Pershing IIs and GLCMs provide the Americans with limited nuclear options, delivered from European territory, against Soviet command, control, and communications facilities.[27] Certainly, the Soviets acknowledge that the Americans believe they will have new options. As V. Nekrasov has argued:

> There is no doubt that the USA intends its missiles to be permanently stationed on this side of the Atlantic, for it sees the European continent as a theatre of possible hostilities lying close to the vital centres of the Soviet Union. The Pentagon believes it is a bridgehead that may witness the first exchange of nuclear strikes that would make the USSR capitulate thus saving the USA from a crushing retaliatory blow by Soviet strategic forces.[28]

The French and British are also planning a significant modernization of their strategic nuclear forces. (For a Soviet perspective on the scope and nature of this modernization see the article by V. Pustov in appendix B.) The quantity and quality of these modernizations are significant. According to Seignious and Yates, "New British and French nuclear forces will present the Soviet bloc with an entirely new situation...[for] Western Europe will soon process a nuclear triad capable of escalating with the Soviets up to a devastating exchange level."[29] In particular, the growth of the arsenals of the independent nuclear powers in Western Europe presents the Soviets with alternative Western decision-making centers capable of inflicting severe damage on the Soviet Union. As Seignious and Yates have underscored:

> The real danger to the Soviet Union, however, is the vulnerability of its industries and population centers, the so-called soft targets. The destruction of just 34 refineries would halt all gas production in the Soviet Union. Eight well-placed warheads would curtail Soviet copper production. Almost all of the chemical industry would be destroyed in an attack on 25 cities, and the destruction of the city of Pavlodar would deny Moscow 65 percent of its aluminum output. In the eyes of the Kremlin leaders, each British and French SLBM-firing submarine will have, at the very minimum, the ability to destroy the Soviet copper, chemical, and gas-refining industries, as well as almost 70 percent of Soviet aluminum and oil production, while having several warheads each left over to attack Moscow, Murmansk, Leningrad, Stalingrad, and the missile-testing center at Tyuratam.
>
> If Great Britain and France combined and coordinated their forces that are available at any given time,...they could...unquestionably destroy the Soviet Union as a superpower and probably as a viable country.[30]

The combined U.S., French, and British modernizations are significant militarily. From the Soviet point of view, the United States might be able to reestablish a semblance of strategic superiority by enhancing NATO's strategic nuclear capability in the European theater. The American INFs when joined with British and French strategic systems, even if numerically inferior to Soviet systems targeted against Western Europe, could still potentially lead to American strategic superiority, from the Soviet standpoint. If Moscow hopes to fight a conventional war in Europe, the British and French independent nuclear forces represent serious threats. If either a conventional or nuclear war is limited to the European theater, the discharge of American INFs and British and French nuclear weapons could inflict substantial damage on the USSR itself. In fact, the damage could be so great that Moscow would have to terminate the war to preserve what remained of its state and society. Such termination might occur without the use of American or Soviet intercontinental systems. American territory would remain intact. As a result, the Soviet Union might conclude that the greatest threat to the strategic balance involves changes in Western strategic capabilities in the European theater. Moscow might feel that derailing such changes by military deployments, arms control measures, and various political actions is a central priority in the 1980s and 1990s.

The Soviets will also have to contend with what they perceive to be the twin negative political effects of the Alliance's Eurostrategic modernization. On the one hand, the Americans are perceived to be using Euromissile deployments to bind Western Europe more closely to the United States. On the other hand, the potential for an independent West European strategic nuclear force is enhanced by the French and British modernizations. (For a Soviet treatment of the U.S., French, and British modernizations as a whole, see the article by Colonel Belov translated in part in appendix C.)

The Soviets believe the Americans are trying to bind the West Europeans to U.S. interests by deploying Euromissiles. V. Baranovskii has articulated this Soviet perception as follows:

Western Europe is generally aware of the fact that the course of strengthening the role of nuclear weapons in U.S. and NATO global and European strategy is viewed by Washington primarily as one of the most reliable methods of blocking the further development of centrifugal tendencies in U.S.-West European relations and in the North Atlantic Alliance. From time to time reports even get into the press that indisputably attest to the fact that all the clamor about the allies' confidence in the "nuclear guarantees" of their partner across the ocean are deliberately exaggerated first and foremost by the U.S. itself. The initial deployment of new American medium-range nuclear missile weapons in Western Europe is also aimed at cementing the NATO bloc and at binding its West European members even more to Washington's policy.[31]

There are forces in Western Europe that also consider the American Euromissiles to be instruments of coupling. According to V. Mikhnovich:

Both France and England assume that the appearance of American first-strike weapons on European land will allow them to "bind" the U.S. strategic forces to the "defense" of their own interests. In this matter, "the preservation of the American nuclear deterrent potential and its steady modernization is, in our opinion, of critical importance," declared France's Minister of Foreign Affairs Claude Cheysson.[32]

There is little question that the Soviets oppose any coupling effect from the new U.S. missile deployments. What also concerns them is the possibility of the creation of a joint independent nuclear force in

Western Europe under the aegis of Britain and France. The buildup of these two countries' nuclear potential is seen as a critical prerequisite for Western Europe's growing assertiveness within the Western Alliance.[33] The parallel British and French modernizations significantly enhance West European nuclear capability. Hence, the potential for a genuine European nuclear force is increasing (this is discussed more fully in chapter five).

What the Soviets would like to see is U.S.-West European nuclear decoupling, without the further development of Western Europe's own independent nuclear capability. As V. F. Davydov, in the most comprehensive Soviet analysis of the European nuclear force idea to date, articulated the Soviets' desired outcome:

> It appears that supplementing political detente with military detente would allow the United States the possibility of reducing the expenses of its involvement in the so-called "defense" of Western Europe; in turn, for the West European countries the processes of gradually abolishing the NATO structures formed during the "cold war" years would open up the way for decreased dependence on the U.S. without needing a sharp increase in military expenditures, including on nuclear forces, which presupposes the redistribution of the "burden of responsibility" within NATO.[34]

Nonetheless, as William Garner has commented, the West European reaction to decoupling might be quite different. There might be "the acquisition by a confederation of West European powers of an independent nuclear force credible at all levels of combat. Thus not only might a decoupled U.S. be less responsive to the Soviets, but a decoupled Europe might raise new threats fully equal to those they now perceive from the U.S. missiles."[35]

The negative dimension of the Eurostrategic modernization process is well represented by the French challenge to Soviet European security policy. France is in the throes of a militarily significant nuclear modernization program that might well enhance the independence of Europe. This program and its political impact are discussed in the next two chapters.

Notes

1. R. A. Mason, "Military Strategy," in *Soviet Strategy Toward Western Europe,* ed. Edwina Moreton and Gerald Segal (London: George Allen and Unwin, 1984), 166.

2. The argument in this section is shaped by Phillip A. Petersen and Maj. John G. Hines, *The Soviet Conventional Offensive in Europe* (Washington, D.C.: Defense Intelligence Agency, 1983); and James McConnell, "Shifts in Soviet Views on the Proper Focus of Military Development," *World Politics,* forthcoming.

3. *Strategic Survey,* 1981-1982 (London: International Institute for Strategic Studies, 1982), 53.

4. U.S. Department of Defense, *NATO and the Warsaw Pact* (Washington, D.C.: GPO, 1981), 46.

5. Stephen M. Meyer, *Soviet Theatre Nuclear Forces,* part two, Adelphi Paper no. 188 (London: International Institute for Strategic Studies, 1984), 20.

6. *Strategic Survey,* 51.

7. Gregory Treverton, *Nuclear Weapons in Europe,* Adelphi Paper no. 168 (London: International Institute for Strategic Studies, 1981), 9.

8. *NATO and the Warsaw Pact,* 45.

9. Stephen Meyer, *Soviet Theatre Nuclear Forces,* part one, Adelphi Paper no. 187 (London: International Institute for Strategic Studies, 1984), 26, emphasis in original.

10. Jeffrey Record, *NATO's Theater Nuclear Modernization Program* (Washington, D.C.: Institute for Foreign Policy Analysis, 1981), 52.

11. Mason, "Military Strategy," 194-195.

12. Iu. P. Davydov, ed., *SShA-Zapadnaia Evropa: Partnerstvo i sopernichestvo* (Moscow: Nauka, 1978), 226.

13. G. A. Vorontsov, *SShA i Zapadnaia Evropa: Novyi etap otnoshenii* (Moscow: Mezhdunarodnye otnosheniia, 1979), 11.

14. See, for example, V. F. Davydov, T. V. Oberemko and A. I. Utkin, *SShA i zapadnoevropeiskie "tsentry sily"* (Moscow: Nauka, 1978).

15. V. M. Kudrov, "Tri tsentra imperializma: Tendentsii sootnosheniia sil," *SShA,* 1981, no. 10:15-25.

16. O. Bogdanov, "Competition in the Capitalist World," *International Affairs,* 1977, no. 4:43.

17. G. Vorontsov, "SShA i Zapadnaia Evropa v usloviiakh obostreniia mezhdunarodnoi obstanovki," *Mirovaia ekonomika i mezhdunarodnye otnosheniia* [hereinafter *Memo*], 1981, no. 11:41.

18. N. N. Inozemtsev, *Contemporary Capitalism: New Developments and Contradictions* (Moscow: Progress, 1974), 134.

19. V. S. Shein, "SShA i NATO v kontse semidesiatykh," *SShA,* 1979, no. 6:4.

20. *Western Europe Today* (Moscow: Progress, 1980), 160-161.

21. Ibid., 306.

22. See, for example, the following: Maj.Gen. A. Slobodenko, "The Strategy of Nuclear Adventurism," *International Affairs,* 1981, no. 1:26-33; A. Nikonov and R. Faramazian, "Opasnyi kurs nagnetaniia voennoi napriazhennosti," *Memo,* 1981, no. 2:44-69.

23. See, for example, the following: Iu. P. Davydov, "Razriadka, SShA i Zapadnaia Evropa," *SShA,* 1979, no. 3:20-31; Iu. P. Davydov, "Kurs Vashingtona na napriazhennost' i Zapadnaia Evropa," *SShA,* 1980, no. 10:31-42; Ia. Rakhmaninov, "For Peaceful and Fruitful Cooperation in Europe," *International Affairs,* 1980, no. 7:3-9; V. Mikhailov, "The FRG and Peace in Europe," *International Affairs,* 1982, no. 1:3-9.

24. For the concept of the U.S. as an offshore power as a key component of Soviet strategy see Uwe Nerlich, "Change in Europe: A Secular Trend?" *Daedalus,* 110 (Winter 1981):71-103.

25. Colin Gray, "The Arms Race Is About Politics," *Foreign Policy,* no. 9 (Winter 1972-73):117-131.

26. For an overview of Soviet views on the Eurostrategic problem, see William V. Garner, *Soviet Threat Perceptions of NATO's Eurostrategic Missiles* (Paris: Atlantic Institute for International Affairs, 1983).

27. See Lt.Gen. D. Volkogonov, "Strategiia avantiurizma," *Zarubezhnoe voennoe obozrenie,* 1984, no. 5:5-7.

28. V. Nekrasov, "Realities of Modern Europe and 'Atlanticism,'" *International Affairs,* 1984, no. 5:35.

29. George M. Seignious II and Jonathan Paul Yates, "Europe's Nuclear Super-powers," *Foreign Policy,* no. 55 (Summer 1984): 46-47.

30. Ibid., 47-48.

31. V. Baranovsky, "NATO: EES v politike imperializma," *Memo,* 1984, no. 6:37-38.

32. V. Mikhnovich, "Raschety i proschety," *Krasnaia zvezda,* 14 June 1984, 3.

33. A. I. Utkin, "Vashington i problemy NATO," *SShA,* 1983, no. 8:8-9.

34. V. F. Davydov, "Diskussiia o evropeiskikh iadernykh silakh," *SShA,* 1976, no. 3:71-72.

35. Garner, *Soviet Threat Perceptions,* 91.

French Nuclear Forces

The French are planning a significant transformation of their nuclear forces, which will intensify Western and Soviet consideration of the importance of French nuclear forces to the East-West balance. The enhanced salience of the French nuclear forces to the military balance in Europe will make it increasingly difficult for the French to ignore the broader impact of their nuclear forces on European security.

The nuclear modernization is to take place in the 1980s and 1990s. The present force is small and capable of only limited target coverage against Soviet territory and against Warsaw Pact forces that might invade Western territory. By the mid-1990s, the new force structure will be theoretically capable of inflicting massive, widespread destruction on the Soviet Union and on specific military targets in Eastern Europe.

The French are upgrading both the strategic and the tactical elements of their nuclear arsenal. The major change in strategic weapons will be the increased number of warheads carried by their submarine-launched ballistic missiles (SLBMs), through the use of multiple independently targetable reentry vehicles (MIRVs). MIRVing will bring the number of warheads carried by the strategic submarine force from 80 to 592. The major change in tactical nuclear weapons will be the addition of the capability to attack military targets in Eastern Europe. No longer will the French tactical nuclear force be limited to operating only against Warsaw Pact forces that have invaded Western territory.

French Nuclear Forces Today

French strategic forces now consist of three complementary systems:[1] six squadrons of strategic bombers, two squadrons of land-based intermediate-range ballistic missiles (IRBMs) and five nuclear-powered ballistic missile submarines (SSBNs). Prime Minister Pierre Mauroy has described the interactive quality of these three systems in the following manner:

Currently, France's nuclear strategic forces consist of three complementary components. First, there are the Mirage IV aircraft, whose flexibility of employment gives the administration possibilities of making certain moves in crisis management. Second, there are the missiles on the Albion plateau which, by virtue of their characteristics and position on national territory, force an adversary to launch a major attack in order to destroy them. Such an attack would indicate the adversary's intentions. Third, there are the missile-firing nuclear submarines. By virtue of their invulnerability on the open sea and the permanent threat that they constitute..., they represent a second-strike force, turning national territory into a sanctuary.[2]

The French nuclear force as of 1983 is described in table 3.1.

The Mirage IV, the first element of the French strategic forces to become operational, went into service in October 1964; by 1966, there were 42 of them.[3] This bomber can reach deep into Soviet territory with midair refueling by the KC-135 tanker aircraft that France purchased from the United States in the mid-1960s.

The Mirage IV has undergone several modifications. Originally designed as a high-altitude bomber, it was later adapted for a low-level role. The Mirage IV has since been modified with the addition of advanced electronic-countermeasures equipment, to enhance its ability to penetrate Soviet air defenses.

The Mirage IV carries a payload of two 70-kiloton bombs (the AN-22). These bombs are stocked at nine bases of the Forces Aériennes Stratégiques (FAS). Although some of these bases are used only occasionally by the FAS, their dispersal throughout France requires an adversary who wishes to neutralize the air arm to mount a major strike against French territory.

The second element of the French strategic triad is the small force of 18 IRBMs. The French first deployed the S-2 IRBM in 1971. The 18 S-2s were two-stage, solid-propellant missiles, each carrying a single 150-kiloton warhead for a maximum range of 2,750 kilometers. In 1980 and 1981 the S-2 was replaced by the S-3. The S-3, also with two stages, carries a heavier payload (1 megaton) for a greater distance (more than 3,000 kilometers). *Jane's* credits it with "a hardened thermonuclear charge and a re-entry vehicle which is hardened also against the effects of a high altitude nuclear explosion from an ABM."[4]

The 18 S-3s are located on the Albion Plateau in southeastern France because, according to the commandant of the FAS, "the terrain features permitted the building of missile silos and there was low population density." The silos are from 3 to 8 kilometers apart. Each

TABLE 3.1
FRENCH NUCLEAR FORCES, 1983

Delivery Mode	Weapon System		Range[a] (km)	Warhead Type	Payload (kt)
	Number	Type			
Land-based aircraft:					
Strategic bombers	34	Mirage IVA	1,500	AN-22	70
Tankers	11	KC-135	--	--	--
Tactical strike	45	Jaguar	720	AN-52	15
aircraft	30	Mirage IIIE.	800	AN-52	15
Land-based missiles:					
IRBMs	18	S-3	3,000	single	1,000
SRBMs	42	Pluton	120	single	15-25
Sea-based:					
Carrier-based	36	Super Etendard	650	AN-52	15
aviation	80	M-20	3,000	single	1,000
SSBNs (5)	(16 each)				

Sources: *The Military Balance, 1983-84* (London: International Institute for Strategic Studies, 1983), 31-33; *Connaissance de l'histoire* (July-August 1980).
[a]Hi-low-hi flight profile.

squadron of nine is controlled by a single command post; the two command posts are 25 kilometers apart. The targets are, of course, preprogrammed into the missiles, but they can be changed in 1 minute for a single missile or in 5 minutes for all 18.[6] All 18 missiles can be launched within 7 minutes after authorization to fire is received.[7]

The IRBMs serve as indicators of the Soviet Union's intentions toward France in wartime. According to one French government report, "the Albion Plateau is vulnerable to a first strike. The *signature* of such an attack would, however, justify the use of the strategic nuclear forces against the aggressor."[8] It has been estimated that destruction of the Albion Plateau would require a 20-megaton attack.[9] According to experts in the French Ministry of Defense, every silo on the Albion Plateau can resist the explosion of a 1-megaton warhead at a distance of 500 meters.[10]

The third and most important element of the triad is the strategic submarine force. The French now deploy five Redoutable-class SSBNs. Since January 1983, three of them have been on station at all times.[11]

The Redoutable-class submarine carries 16 SLBMs, or as the French call them, *mer-sol balistiques stratégiques* (MSBS). The first MSBS, the M-1, was tested initially in 1964. It went into service in 1971 and was phased out in favor of the M-2 in 1974. By 1977, the M-2 was supplanted by the M-20. The first SSBNs, or *sous-marins nucléaires lanceurs d'engins* (SNLEs), were the *Redoutable* and the *Terrible*, which entered service between 1971 and 1973, armed with 16 M-1 missiles each. In 1974 the *Foudroyant* introduced the M-2, followed by the the *Indomptable* in 1977. All four SSBNs have since been rearmed with the M-20. A fifth boat, the *Tonnant*, was launched in 1976 and received the M-20 missile in 1980. A sixth, the *Inflexible*, which is scheduled for deployment in 1985, is described in the next section. The life cycles for these SSBNs are shown in table 3.2.

In addition to a thermonuclear warhead, the M-20 program introduced improved aids for penetrating antimissile defenses. Other technical improvements enhanced the range, flight envelope, and rate of fire of the missile system.[12]

Before January 1983, when the number of SSBNs on patrol was increased from two to three, an authoritative French source said that the operational cycle for each SSBN was more than 200 ship days.[13] Each year, each SSBN made two sea patrols of 9 to 10 weeks apiece, with a 4-week period of physical reconditioning at the submarine base at Ile Longue (near Brest) in north western France. Each SSBN is served by two alternating crews. A French submariner goes on an

TABLE 3.2
ESTIMATED LIFE CYCLES FOR FRENCH SSBNs

SSBN	Hull Number	Laid Down	Operational	Approximate End of Service Life
Le Redoutable	S611	1964	1971	1997
Le Terrible	S612	1967	1973	1999
Le Foudroyant	S610	1969	1974	2002
L'Indomptable	S613	1971	1976	2004
Le Tonnant	S614	1974	1980	2008
L'Inflexible	S615	1980	1985	2012

Source: *Jane's Fighting Ships, 1983-84* (London: Jane's Publishing Co., 1984), 155.

average of four patrols on SSBNs during his service. Several French naval officers have been on as many as 12 patrols.

The Redoutable-class SSBN displaces 8,000 tons surfaced and 8,940 tons submerged and can reach a speed of 20 knots surfaced and 25 knots submerged. It carries a crew of 135 men (including 15 officers), 16 SLBMs, and 18 torpedoes and has a diving depth of 900 feet under normal operating conditions. The reactor, of the natural-water-cooled type, uses enriched uranium and drives two twin turbines and two turbo-alternators.[14]

The French Oceanic Strategic Force (FOST) consists of the five operational SSBNs, an experimental submarine (the *Gymnote*), the operational base at Ile Longue, and a number of command posts (CPs) and signaling stations.[15] The ALFOST (admiral in charge of the FOST) operates from a command post at Houilles, 10 kilometers northwest of Paris. Very-low-frequency (VLF) transmission links are used to communicate directly from Houilles to the Rosnay communication post in northwestern France.

The antennas in this system are vulnerable to attack, but ALFOST can turn to low-frequency (LF) or high-frequency (HF) channels.[16]

One French source has described the communication system with the SSBNs as follows:

> Communications with the SNLEs are normally one-way: the SNLE has to remain entirely mute so as not to risk revealing its position, while it continually receives operational or personal messages. The FOST command, in its command post--protected against nuclear attack--at Houilles in the Yvelines, possesses for these communications its own radio-transmission network with the Kerlouan station, near Brest, and the Rosnay (Indres) station, specially designed for communications with the submerged SNLEs. This Rosnay station, which cost about 280 million francs, is equipped with two very-long-range (about 9,000-kilometer), 580-kilowatt transmitters. It uses very-low-frequency (14 to 23 kilohertz) transmission by "surface waves" that propagate in the ground and in water (to a depth of about 10 meters). To pick up these transmissions, the SNLEs trail a special antenna with an underwater float at the end.[17]

Use of the strategic forces can be ordered only by the President of France (see figure 3.1). The command and control system operates through several key links.

The Centre Opérationnel de la Défense Aérienne (CODA) decides when an attack is imminent and conveys this assessment to the Centre de l'Opérations des Forces Aériennes Stratégiques (COFAS), at Taverny. The COFAS, in turn, informs the President. When the decision to execute a strategic strike has been made, the COFAS sends operational orders to the two command posts at the Albion Plateau and to the Mirage IV bomber squadrons. In addition, the ALFOST is ordered to carry out an SLBM attack. He sends his orders through the operations center at Houilles, which communicates directly with the SSBNs on patrol.[18] The French now rely mainly on land links to connect the strategic decision-makers.[19] One French source has described the procedure for executing a strategic submarine attack:

> To enable the President of the Republic to order the FNS [Strategic Nuclear Force] into action, the FOST makes sure that direct communications between the President and the nuclear submarines are always available. The admiral commanding the Strategic Naval Force has a number of command posts and signaling stations to help meet his own operational and organic responsibilities.
>
> The main command post is installed in a protected zone of the Commandant Mille Centre, at the junction of the communes of Houilles and Carrières-sur-Seine, old quarries that the German navy used as a shop for assembling submarine torpedoes. It is installed in a specially protected concrete structure. The other command posts are located with the commanders in chief for the Atlantic and the Mediterranean.
>
> Especially because of the presence of French air and naval forces in all theaters, the command posts add information--in particular intelligence about foreign forces at sea--and transmit it to the submarines. The command posts are linked to the signaling stations, one of which is at Rosnay in the Indre.[20]

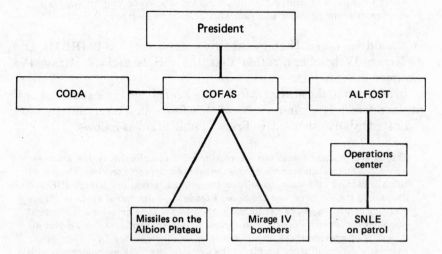

Source: *Le Monde,* 19 May 1980.

Fig. 3.1. Chain of Command, French Strategic Forces.

How much destruction could the present strategic forces inflict? One French government report, released in 1980, estimated that the French strategic forces would have the following effects:

On the basis of the effects of the strike on Hiroshima, the combined strike delivered by 3 submarines, 9 S-3 missiles, and 37 Mirage IV aircraft (assuming that all our equipment is available and that all our warheads hit their targets) would be capable of killing 20 million individuals, wounding an equivalent number, and causing major disorganization of enemy activities nationwide.[21]

It should be noted that France now deploys 18 S-3 IRBMs and 34 Mirage IV bombers, rather than the 9 S-3s and 37 Mirage IVs assumed in the report.

In addition to the strategic force, the French deploy a small tactical nuclear force. The components of this force and their purpose are indicated by an authoritative French publication as follows:

The tactical nuclear forces are an indispensable complement to the strategic forces. The tactical nuclear warhead is the same for the three services. The AN-52 bomb is carried by Pluton missiles in the ground forces, the Mirage IIIE and Jaguars in the air force, and the Super Etendards in the naval air force. These weapons can be used against forces in the combat zone or behind it. Tactical nuclear weapons are important in enhancing the conventional ground and air forces. They provide these classic forces with considerable firepower. They exercise a major influence simply by the threat of their use in conjunction with conventional weapons. Because the tactical weapons are weapons of deterrence, their use can be decided upon only by the highest national authority, the head of state. Their use would be a key political action by which France advertises in advance its willingness to use strategic weapons.[22]

The tactical forces rely mainly on the AN-52 warhead, which is estimated at 15 kilotons. The AN-51, an alternative warhead with a 25-kiloton capability, is available primarily for the Pluton missile. The AN-52 would be used near the main battle area; the AN-51 is intended for use in an enemy's rear area.[23]

The Pluton short-range missile was first deployed in 1974. Currently there are 42 Pluton launchers deployed in five regiments. The Pluton launchers can be reloaded and prepared to fire a second time in less than 30 minutes. The weapon has a range of up to 120 kilometers with a circular error probable (CEP) of 150 to 300 meters, depending on range. The Pluton is installed on, and fired from, the AMX-30 tank chassis, with the missile container used as a launcher ramp. The missile and warhead are supplied separately to units in the field. When deployed, the Plutons in each regiment are dispersed throughout the terrain, more than 15 kilometers apart. The target can be set 3 minutes before firing.[24]

The deployment of the Pluton with French conventional forces has the advantage of deterring the adversary from massing his forces. Nonetheless, the presence of the Pluton compels the conventional forces to commit assets to defending it, assets that could be contributing to the conventional military effort. Also, the Pluton's short range means that it would be used only against Warsaw Pact forces already occupying West German territory.

The French tactical land-based aircraft would be used primarily in conjunction with the Plutons in attacking invading Warsaw Pact forces in West Germany. The French currently deploy 45 Jaguars and 30 Mirage IIIs to carry out the tactical nuclear ground attack mission. The three squadrons of Jaguars and two of Mirage IIIs could, however, be used to carry out strikes at the enemy's rear, given the 720-kilometer combat range of the Jaguar and the 800-kilometer combat range of the Mirage III.[25]

In addition, the two French aircraft carriers currently have 36 Super Etendard strike aircraft available for a tactical nuclear mission. The *Clemenceau* was refitted in 1978 to accommodate tactical nuclear weapons. The *Foch* underwent a similar retrofit from July 1980 to August 1981. Each aircraft carrier can carry 40 aircraft and will receive additional Super Etendards in the future. Sea-based tactical air power provides the French with a nuclear strike force against targets on land or at sea. An authoritative French publication has indicated the roles for this component of the strike force:

[This force]...gives the government the means to deal with an aggressor threatening national territory from the sea, it multiplies the axis of attack against the enemy's forces of invasion by providing the possibility of conducting strikes from the sea...and it assures the government of the possibility of resisting an adversary's nuclear blackmail during a major maritime crisis affecting the vital interests of the nation.[26]

The last role implies that the French have in mind the possibility of adversaries other than the Soviets, notably a Third World nuclear power that might attempt nuclear blackmail.

The role of the three components of the tactical nuclear arsenal--ground forces and land-based and sea-based air forces--is to provide enhanced credibility to the strategic deterrent. Prime Minister Mauroy has defined the relationship between strategic and tactical nuclear weapons as follows:

Despite permanent adaptation and modernization, strategic nuclear deterrence may turn out to be insufficient itself or it may be outflanked. To prevent this outflanking, the nuclear strategic forces must be joined by the conventional forces, which have been upgraded with tactical nuclear weapons. The purpose of tactical nuclear weapons thus is to restore deterrence on the strategic level. Their employment would signify the determination of the President of the Republic to go all the way and, if necessary, to resort to the use of nuclear weapons aimed at the population. This does not mean that tactical nuclear weapons should be used to win a battle but instead, with the help of these tactical nuclear weapons, in a credible fashion to brandish the strategic nuclear threat if an armed conflict should in spite of everything be triggered by the aggressor in the European theater.[27]

The French are modernizing each element of their nuclear deterrent, strategic and tactical, precisely to enhance the credibility of both.

The French Nuclear Modernization Program

In mid-1983 the French government passed its most recent 5-year military plan. The Military Program Law for 1984 to 1988 provides a framework for strategic planning that is a good guide to French intentions and a realistic indicator of future military capabilities. The nuclear force modernization projected here is drawn from this 5-year plan and from public discussion of the plan before and after its promulgation.[28]

The French plan a significant enhancement of the sea-based strategic deterrent. Two SSBNs are to be added to the FOST, and almost the entire SSBN force will be fitted or retrofitted with MIRVed SLBMs.

The first SSBN to be added will be the *Inflexible* in 1985.[29] The *Inflexible* is a modification of the Redoutable-class SSBN. The *Inflexible* will be the first French submarine to carry a MIRVed SLBM (the M-4). This 16-tube SSBN is expected to be in service until 2012.

The second SSBN to be added will be the first of a completely new class. According to Defense Minister Hernu, the new class will be quieter, have a more effective type of metal hull, and be able to operate at greater depths. It is also hoped that this new SSBN will carry a new generation of MIRVed SLBMs (the M-5).[30] The first unit of the new class is expected to be operational in 1994 with a service life extending to 2020. This SSBN may carry more than the 16 tubes of the current generation.

The two new SSBNs will give the French a total of seven. But this will not be a seven-boat force for long. Given French estimates that the new-generation SSBN will come on line in 1994, it will be available only 3 years before the scheduled retirement in 1997 of the initial Redoutable-class unit. Although the government refers to the new-generation SSBN as the "seventh" submarine, it would be more accurate to describe it as the sixth operational SSBN.[31]

The French are unlikely to have in operation more than six or seven SSBNs in any case. The current base at Ile Longue can support no more than seven SSBNs. Adding more would require constructing a second base. In addition, the French Navy is a medium-sized force, which operates surface, as well as submarine, forces. Increasing the number of submarines would require the French Navy to limit its surface missions, given constraints on manpower and funding. Also, adding more SLBM tubes in the context of the MIRVing trend would give France more than a minimum assured-destruction force, something the French simply do not wish to have.

The first French SLBM capable of carrying multiple warheads will be the M-4, a three-stage missile. The first stage has a metal casing, and the other two motors have casings wound of Kevlar material produced in the United States.[32] The M-4 program began in earnest in 1974. Initially, the M-4 was to carry three warheads not capable of being independently targeted, but when it is deployed in 1985, the missile will carry six warheads (150 kilotons each) that can be independently targeted.[33] The M-4 has a much longer range than the M-20. The range is generally described as being more than 4,000 kilometers, but one authoritative report indicates that "under certain conditions its range is nearly 6,000 kilometers."[34] Another French source has reported that the 6,000-kilometer range is attained when fewer warheads are carried by the SLBM.[35] A much less authoritative report speculated that the M-4 in one test had a CEP of 300 meters when fired at maximum range.[36] The M-4 has a 20-minute flight time to target with a peak altitude of 800 kilometers.[37] The warheads of the M-4 have been "rendered as little sensitive as possible to electronic countermeasures and anti-missile missiles."[38]

The increased range of the M-4 is of major significance to the FOST. The 4,000-kilometer minimum range will allow the FOST to strike Moscow from the Norwegian Sea. A 6,000-kilometer maximum range would allow it to operate outside the Greenland-Iceland-United Kingdom Gap and still threaten Moscow. Another possibility is using waters close to French shores as a bastion to protect French submarines against Soviet ASW efforts.

The M-4 was first deployed on the Inflexible in 1984 and will become operational in 1985. "The general design of the M-4 was defined by the necessity of introducing the operational innovations but without extensively modifying the structure of the existing SSBNs."[39] An extensive retrofit program is planned in which all but the original Redoutable-class SSBN will carry M-4s.[40] This program is shown in table 3.3.

TABLE 3.3
M-4 RETROFIT PROGRAM

SSBN	Operational with M-4s	End of SSBN's Service Life
Le Tonnant	1987	2008
L'Indomptable	1989	2004
Le Terrible	1990	1999
Le Foudroyant	1992	2002

The new class of SSBN that is to become operational in the mid-1990s is designed to carry a new generation of SLBM, the M-5. This SLBM will carry at least six warheads and will be spin-stabilized to improve its ability to penetrate ballistic missile defenses (BMD).[41] A major French concern throughout the SLBM modernization program has been, and will continue to be, the ability of its SLBMs to penetrate Soviet BMD. As French Army Chief of Staff General Lacaze noted, "This significant augmentation of our numbers of weapons is necessary throughout the next 20 years to allow us to deal with the danger that will be presented by the development of antiballistic missile systems of the new generation."[42]

The number of French SLBM warheads will jump dramatically in the next 10 years. Currently, the FOST has a maximum of 80 SLBM warheads available. By the mid-1990s, a maximum of approximately 600 warheads will be available (see table 3.4).

Although the expansion of the striking power of the FOST is the most significant element of the French strategic modernization effort, there are plans to deploy a mobile land-based IRBM as well. The SX is

TABLE 3.4
FRENCH SLBM WARHEADS

	1983	1985	1987	1989	1990	1992	1994
Warheads on M-20 SLBMs	80	80	64	48	32	16	16
Warheads on M-4 SLBMs	--	96	192	288	384	480	480
Warheads on M-5 SLBMs	--	--	--	--	--	--	96+
Total	80	176	256	336	416	496	592+

currently under development and is expected to be deployed in 1996. The SX will be transportable over roads and will be dispersed in times of crisis to enhance its survivability.[43] The SX will have a range of 3,000 to 4,000 kilometers, which would allow it to reach targets in the Soviet Union almost up to the Urals. Both the transporter-erector-launchers and the missiles are to be transportable by air.[44] The deployment figures for the SX have not yet been announced.

The SX will replace the Mirage IV force, which will be retired by 1996.[45] It is not, however, clear whether the SX will also replace the fixed-site IRBMs. It has been announced that the 18 S-3s will remain in service until 1996, but the French government has never linked SX deployment with S-3 retirement.[46] If the government considers the function of the Albion Plateau really to be providing indication of a general Soviet attack, then the fixed-site IRBMs may be kept in service, albeit modernized. Because the S-3 is a version of the M-20, it could be expected that a land-based version of the MIRVed M-4 would be a logical follow-on system.[47]

Besides these significant increases to their strategic nuclear arsenal, the French plan to create--really for the first time--a tactical nuclear force capable of attacking military targets in Eastern Europe. There will be two prongs to the French tactical nuclear force in the future--the Hades ground-launched missile and the ASMP air-

launched missile. The two prongs will be combined under the direction
of a single tactical nuclear command placed directly under the French
Chief of Staff.

The Hades will replace the Pluton. It has a longer range
(350 kilometers) and a larger warhead (20 to 60 kilotons) than the
Pluton.[48] The French plan to deploy four or five squadrons of Hades,
with the first squadron to be operational in 1992.[49] One report
indicates that each Hades transporter-erector-launcher (TEL) will
carry two missiles and that as many as 100 TELs will be deployed.[50]
The Hades will also be capable of carrying an enhanced radiation, or
neutron, warhead, although the political decision on whether it will do
so has not yet been made.[51]

The increased range of the Hades will allow it to strike military
targets in East Germany or Czechoslovakia from France. It appears
that the French envisage striking fixed military targets, such as
airfields and C^3 facilities, or geographical choke points with this
weapon.[52] The Hades, in other words, unlike the Pluton, will be able
to strike military targets in Eastern Europe. Clearly, West German
sensitivities on the issue of French tactical nuclear weapons have
been taken into consideration. One French newspaper report referred
to the Hades as the "diplomatic missile."[53]

The deployment of the Hades will have an important impact on
French conventional military forces as well. One French government
report went so far as to characterize the new tactical ground forces as
being "decoupled" from the operations of the conventional forces.[54]
Whereas the conventional forces would use the Pluton as a key
element of their operations in West Germany, with the retirement of
the Pluton, they will be left to operate in closer cooperation with
NATO forces in fighting Warsaw Pact forces.[55]

A good descripton of the changes in the conventional military
situation created in part by the Hades deployment has been provided
by Jacques Isnard of *Le Monde*.

Officials in the Elysée Palace as well as in the Ministry of Defense believe that
technological advances expected in certain weapon systems--the Hades nuclear
missile and antitank helicopters--make it possible to reconcile two objectives that
have long seemed contradictory. French Army combat forces stationed on both
sides of the Rhine are currently organized essentially into two (or three) corps
consisting of a total of seven (or eight) armored divisons reinforced by infantry
divisions, and serving as a screen for five nuclear artillery regiments.... The
tank's relative mobility and the Pluton's 120-kilometer range give these
combined forces, known as the First Army, capabilities that actually leave a
potential enemy guessing about the geographical limits within which these forces
may be committed.

But in reality it's either one thing or the other. Either the chief of state, wanting to fulfill his obligations to the Alliance, decides to move his First Army forward--including Pluton units which move along with it--into West German territory. At the same time, he must require his allies to give him sufficient advance notice to assemble the French forces. And above all, he must agree to delegate to subordinate commands authority to fire missiles dispersed throughout the combat area, and this at the risk of impairing the national strategy of deterrence, which implies centralized launching of an immediate and massive retaliatory strike. Or else, this same chief of state decides to defend solely the national sanctuary in the--almost neutralist or isolationist--belief that France's vital interests stop at the Rhine. In so doing, he deviates from his obligations to the Alliance at the risk of having to withdraw into France without fighting--if he has the time--the three French armored divisions stationed in the FRG.[56]

The deployment of the Hades will change the situation because there will be no need to move the Hades into West Germany to support French First Army operations in Central Europe. In addition, the French are creating a rapid action force of 47,000 men and new helicopter forces. The mobility of these forces would enable them to advance and to meet an attack toward West Germany's eastern borders. According to Isnard, deployment of the Hades and the formation of the rapid action force will create a more flexible situation for French decision-makers.

Deployment and disposition of these forces can be tailored, as the chief of state sees fit, to all major contingencies, whether the First Army is still not up to full strength and is being manned, equipped, and prepared to intervene, or even whether there are no plans to commit that field army in the immediate future, in which case the Hades missiles are aimed, from positions in France and under French command, at enemy targets so as to support the counteroffensive by allied forces in Central Europe. The threat of Hades employment can thus be divorced from operational engagement of the First Army--a radically different posture from the one allowed by the Pluton missile--thereby enhancing the credibility of France's engagement alongside its allies from the very first moment of a crisis or conflict. At the same time, this posture increases the enemy's perplexity about French intentions.[57]

The second prong of the French tactical nuclear modernization program is the ASMP, the French version of the U.S. short-range attack missile (SRAM).[58] The ASMP can attain a speed of Mach 3 and has a range of 100 kilometers at low altitude and 300 kilometers at high altitude. It has a preprogrammed inertial guidance system. Most sources indicate that the ASMP will carry a 100- to 150-kiloton warhead, although Defense Minister Hernu has indicated that it will also be capable of carrying a 300-kiloton warhead.[59] The French appear to have plans for a successor to the ASMP. They plan to develop an attack missile (the ASLP) with longer range and improved guidance.[60] This could be the cruise missile alternative for the SX or simply an additional new element for French strategic forces.

The ASMP will be carried by three airborne platforms.[61] Eighteen Mirage IVs will be fitted with ASMPs in the mid-1980s and will remain in service until the SX is deployed. In addition, the ASMP will become the main nuclear armament of the Mirage 2000N force, which will be deployed in the 1980s and 1990s. The French plan to replace the current force of Mirage IIIs and Jaguars with 85 Mirage 2000Ns by the early 1990s (36 by 1988 and 49 after 1988). The Mirage 2000N has a longer range than the Mirage III (one-third greater) and improved avionics (a look-down, shoot-down capability). Although considered a tactical aircraft, the Mirage 2000 has nearly the range of the Mirage IV. The ASMP will also be carried by the Super Etendard aircraft aboard the two aircraft carriers. Forty-three Super Etendards will be armed with the ASMP by 1988, with 10 more planes to be so armed later.

The Hades and the ASMP will be under the direction of a newly created tactical nuclear command.[62] This command is placed directly under the chief of staff of the army. The creation of this new command, coupled with the ability to operate tactical forces solely on French territory, clearly increases the ability of decision-makers to control the use of these weapons.

The planned transformation of France's strategic and tactical nuclear forces is summarized in table 3.5.

Besides increasing the firepower of their nuclear forces, the French plan to enhance the credibility of their deterrent by other means. The French ASW capability will be enhanced by the deployment of six additional nuclear-powered attack submarines (SSNs) by 1992 for a total of eight. The first French SSN became operational in 1982, and the second began sea trials in 1981. The French will also deploy 16 second-generation Atlantique maritime patrol aircraft, which will be available to provide protection for SSBNs.[63] The French are also planning to enhance their command, control, and communications (C^3) systems by deploying four airborne platforms for the ASTARTE system, which is designed to transmit orders in conditions of severe electromagnetic pulse caused by high-altitude thermonuclear explosions.[64] General Lacaze has argued that deploying the ASTARTE system is as important as building additional SSBNs in enhancing the credibility of the French nuclear deterrent.[65]

TABLE 3.5
TRANSFORMATION OF FRENCH NUCLEAR FORCES,
1980s-1990s

1983	1988	Early to Mid-1990s
5 SSBNs with M-20s	+1 SSBN +1 SSBN retrofit with M4s	1 SSBN with M-20s 5 SSBNs with M-4s 1 SSBN with M-5s
18 S-3s	no change	MIRVed IRBMS?
34 Mirage IVs	18 Mirage IVs with ASMPs	100 SX IRBMS
42 Plutons	no change	100 Hades
36 Super Etendards	+7 Super Etendards (all 43 with ASMPs)	53 Super Etendards with ASMPs
45 Jaguars 30 Mirage IIIs	+36 Mirage 2000Ns with ASMPs	85 Mirage 2000Ns with ASMPs

The Transformation of French Nuclear Forces

The quantity of French nuclear forces will be significantly increased by the modernization program. The most dramatic increase will be in submarine warheads, as the current force of 80 M-20s is replaced in the mid-1990s by a mixed force of 480 M-4s, at least 96 M-5s, and possibly 16 M-20s. Table 3.6 shows a five-fold increase in strategic warheads, with a more modest increase of less than 100 tactical warheads. These figures are only rough approximations, however, because of incomplete data about the new systems' characteristics and uncertainty about final deployment figures.

The quality of the French nuclear force structure will be enhanced as well. Table 3.7 provides some sense of the qualitative improvements, expressed in terms of range and payload. The SLBM force will have greater range, which in turn will enhance the survivability of French SSBNs. They will be able to operate either in a bastion near

France or much further from the European continent. The IRBM force will become more survivable and have greater range with the deployment of the SX. The tactical forces will have greater range, payload, and survivability.

TABLE 3.6
WARHEADS CARRIED BY FRENCH NUCLEAR FORCES

Warheads	1983	Mid-1990s
Strategic		
Sea-based	80	592
Land-based	52	100[a]
Total	132	692
Tactical		
Sea-based	36	53
Land-based[b]	117	185
Total	153	238
Total warheads	285	930

[a]Assuming deployment of 100 SX missiles and the complete phasing out of land- based IRBMs.
[b]Assuming the Pluton will be unable to fire its reload.

The Hades has three times the range of the Pluton and more than double its payload and does not have to operate from West Germany. The ASMP program, coupled with the Mirage 2000N deployment, will increase the payload (by three to ten times) and the survivability (by removing the need to fly directly over the target) of the French tactical air force dedicated to the nuclear mission.

A very important change will take place in the relationship between the tactical and strategic forces. To the extent that France is able to enhance the survivability of its SSBN force, it increases the significance of the French tactical nuclear arm. The Soviets are not in a position to preempt the French tactical nuclear forces--to be located

TABLE 3.7
RANGE AND PAYLOAD OF FRENCH NUCLEAR SYSTEMS

Weapon System	Range (km)	Payload (kt)
SLBMs		
M-20	3,000	1,000
M-4	4,000-6,000	150
M-5	unknown	unknown
IRBMs		
S-2	2,750	150
S-3	3,500	1,000
SX	3,000-4,000	unknown
Strategic bombers		
Mirage IVA	1,500[a]	70[b]
Tactical ground systems		
Pluton	120	15-25
Hades	350	20-60
Tactical air systems		
Jaguar	720[a]	30[c]
Mirage IIIE	800[a]	30[c]
Mirage 2000N	1200[a]	
+ ASMP	+ 100	100-300
Super Etendard	720[a]	30[c]
+ ASMP	+100	100-300

Source: *The Military Balance, 1983-1984*. (London: International Institute for Strategic Studies, 1983), 31-33.
[a]Combat radius with normal payload and flight profile (hi-lo-hi) without refueling but with external fuel tanks.
[b]One AN-22 bomb.
[c]Two AN-52 bombs.

solely on French soil--without the threat of massive retaliation against Soviet cities by the SSBN and IRBM forces. The tactical nuclear forces in turn enhance the credibility of the strategic forces. Even if the Soviets have some degree of confidence in reducing the level of damage to be expected from a French strategic response, they have to be concerned with a massive French tactical strike against their forces in Eastern Europe.

In short, the French are engaging in a significant nuclear modernization program. The Soviets clearly hope that the increased military capability of France's nuclear forces will not be used politically by French leaders to strengthen France's role in European security. It is the political role of French nuclear forces that will be considered next.

Notes

1. *Armées d'aujourd'hui*, July-August 1982, 8.

2. Pierre Mauroy, "La Cohérence d'une politique de défense," *Défense nationale*, October 1981, 13.

3. The information on the Mirage IV has been taken from "Les Forces nucléaires françaises," *Connaissance de l'histoire*, July-August 1980, 37-50.

4. *Jane's Weapon Systems, 1981-1982* (London: Jane's Publishing Co., 1981), 3.

5. "Les Forces nucléaires françaises," 49.

6. Ibid., 52-57.

7. *Christian Science Monitor*, 19 July 1983.

8. *Rapport fait au nom de la Commission de la défense nationale et des forces armées* (Paris: Assemblée nationale, 18 May 1983), 49, emphasis in original.

9. *Le Monde*, 23 May 1980.

10. *Le Nouveau Journal*, 23 May 1980. See also *New York Times*, 9 May 1983.

11. *Le Monde*, 13 December 1982.

12. "The French Navy's SSBNs," *Defence* 12 (August 1981): 561.

13. Capt. Cazenave, *Cols bleus*, 2 October 1982, 5-8.

14. "Les Forces nucléaires françaises," 18-27.

15. *Armées d'aujourd'hui*, July-August 1982, 8.

16. "Les Forces nucléaires françaises," 18-27.

17. Paul Antony, "FOST," *La Recherche*, October 1981, 1151.

18. *Le Monde*, 19 May 1980.

19. "Les Forces nucléaires françaises," 47-50.

20. Cazenave, *Cols bleus*, 8.

21. *Le Monde*, 26-27 October 1980.

22. *Armées d'aujourd'hui*, July-August 1982, 8.

23. *Jane's Weapon Systems, 1981-1982*, 42.

24. The material in this and the following paragraph was taken from Ibid. and "Les Forces nucléaires françaises," 6-9.

25. "Les Forces nucléaires françaises," 28-32.

26. *Armées d'aujourd'hui*, July-August 1982, 16.

27. Pierre Mauroy, "La Cohérence d'une politique de défense," 14.

28. See *Projet de loi portant de la programmation militaire pour les années 1984-1988* (Paris: Assemblée nationale, 21 April 1983); *Rapport de la Commission de la défense nationale; Rapport fait au nom de la Commission des affaires étrangères, de la défense et des forces armées sur le projet de loi...programmation militaire pour les années 1984-1988* (Paris: Senat, 9 June 1983).

29. *Le Matin*, 24 June 1982.

30. *Le Monde*, 6 December 1981.

31. *Rapport de la Commission des affaires étrangères*, 19.

32. *Jane's Weapon Systems, 1981-1982*, 4.

33. According to the Director of the Ballistic and Space Division of Aérospatiale, the six M-4 warheads are capable of being "...guided independently to distinct targets or arriving spaced at a single target." *Air et cosmos*, 11 June 1983, 105.

34. *Rapport de la Commission de la défense nationale*, 50.

35. *Air et cosmos*, 11 June 1983, 105.

36. *Le Figaro*, 4 December 1980.

37. Antony, "FOST," 1152.

38. "Les Forces nucléaires françaises," 42.

39. Antony, "FOST," 1152.

40. *Le Monde*, 24 June 1982.

41. *Le Monde*, 6 December 1981.

42. Gen. Lacaze, "Politique de défense et stratégie militaire de la France," *Défense nationale*, June 1983, 16.

43. *Le Matin*, 16 November 1981.

44. *Rapport de la Commission de la défense nationale*, 50.

45. *Le Monde*, 16-17 May 1982.

46. *Rapport de la Commission de la défense nationale*, 49.

47. *Washington Times*, 11 August 1983, 3.

48. Emmanuel Gepeyre, "L'Armament nucléaire dans l'armée de terre," *Défense nationale*, July 1982, 165-168; *Le Monde*, 15-16 November 1981.

49. *Rapport de la Commission de la défense nationale*, 5.

50. *Le Monde*, 6 May 1981.

51. *Le Matin*, 16 January 1981; *Le Monde*, 22 April 1983.

52. *Rapport de la Commission de la défense nationale*, 83.

53. *Le Nouveau Journal*, 19 October 1982.

54. *Rapport de la Commission des affaires étrangères*, 27.

55. *Le Monde*, 25 June 1983.

56. *Le Monde*, 16 December 1982.

57. Ibid.

58. *Aéronautique et l'astronautique*, 1981, no. 6: 25-28; *Jane's Weapon Systems, 1981-1982*, 154.

59. *Le Monde*, 22-23 November 1981.

60. Germain Chambost, "The Mirage 2000," *International Defense Review* 12 (1979): 1141.

61. *Projet de loi*, 14-15.

62. *Rapport de la Commission des affaires étrangères*, 28-29.

63. *Rapport de la Commission de la défense nationale*, 59-60.

64. Ibid.

65. Lacaze, "Politique de défense," 15.

4

The French Strategic Dilemma

French leaders identify the political purpose of nuclear weapons as the defense of French territory or, at most, of France's "vital interests." But external pressures are making it necessary for France to provide a more explicit definition of the role of French nuclear weapons in the West European security system. This is a basic strategic dilemma for France. The central tension in French doctrine revolves around the traditional emphasis on protecting the national "sanctuary" with nuclear weapons and the growing recognition of the need to include West Germany in the French security concept.

This chapter begins by examining the basic elements of French doctrine, with the focus on identifying the response to a central question: What political purposes are served by French nuclear forces? Next, it looks at the external pressures that are challenging the credibility of the French deterrent and creating a need for change in French doctrine. Then, the resulting French strategic dilemma is identified and discussed, followed by an analysis of the basic French defense options in the 1980s as reflected in the discussions of defense policy in France. Finally, alternative scenarios for the evolution of French defense policy in the 1980s and 1990s are assessed.

French Strategic Doctrine

The central element of the French approach to nuclear weapons is to see them as fundamentally different from conventional weapons in that they pose the gravest questions of life and death. The radical nature of these weapons in terms of the level of destruction they can inflict makes them usable only when the survival of a nation is at stake. Because it would be difficult for any nation, even the United States, to risk its ultimate survival for the sake of its allies, France felt a need to develop an independent nuclear force to defend itself in the nuclear era.[1]

The French have developed a number of ideas associated with their perceived need for an independent national deterrent.[2] First, they believe that possession of nuclear weapons turns French territory into a "sanctuary." If France has the capability to attack Soviet territory directly with nuclear weapons, then France is less likely to be subject to Soviet nuclear strikes. French territory is thereby "sanctuarized" by its possession of nuclear weapons.

Among the Europeans, the French have been most vigorous in casting doubt on U.S. willingness to use its nuclear weapons to implement an extended deterrence strategy. When the French nuclear forces were established in the mid-1960s, Charles de Gaulle coined the phrase that the Americans would not be willing to trade New York for Hamburg in a nuclear war with the Soviet Union. The French have strongly criticized the U.S. concept of flexible response from its inception.[3] They see this concept as simply reflecting U.S. unwillingness to strike Soviet territory with nuclear weapons in light of the Soviets' ability to inflict assured destruction on U.S. territory.

The classic French position equates the use of nuclear weapons with the defense solely of French territory. For example, General Lucien Poirier, a prominent French strategic thinker, has pictured the French security situation as consisting of three circles. Nuclear weapons protect the "national sanctuary," which is the first circle. The second circle encompasses the defense of France's immediate periphery. The third is the defense of France's interests in Africa and the Third World. In Poirier's schema, nuclear weapons are inextricably intertwined with the defense of the first circle but related only ambiguously to the defense of the second circle and not at all to that of the third.[4]

In spite of the independence of French nuclear forces, their credibility as a deterrent rests largely on their ability to operate "behind" U.S. nuclear forces. The preoccupation the Soviets must have with U.S. forces provides a significant "force multiplier" to the French forces. The language of "independence" can obscure the significance of the U.S. deterrent to the credibility of the French deterrent.

A close examination of the substance of three key expressions of French doctrine reveals this significance. First, the French speak of their nuclear forces as the weak deterring the strong. This approach to deterrence is rooted in the clear recognition of the limits within which French strategic power must operate. France can never hope to match the Soviet Union in size or diversity of nuclear forces. In reality, however, the French are really operating vis-à-vis the Soviets in a position of the weak augmenting the strong deterring the strong. The Soviets are deterred in part by recognizing that the damage inflicted by the French might be significant enough to allow the United States to dominate the war termination process. This Soviet concern significantly augments the deterrent effect of French forces.

Second, the French speak of "proportional deterrence." Their strategy is rooted in a capability to inflict damage on the Soviet Union greater than the value to the Soviets of destroying France. Proportional deterrence is credible insofar as French nuclear forces are survivable and can execute a highly destructive second strike. Also underwriting the proportional deterrence strategy is the U.S.-Soviet strategic nuclear standoff. One might be able to conceive of the Soviets' being willing to risk part of their population and industrial assets in order to destroy France in an effort to win a war limited to the European theater. Proportional deterrence would fail in a strictly bilateral Soviet-French exchange. It is more difficult to imagine the Soviets' engaging in a strategic nuclear exchange with France if it would leave Soviet military and economic resources severely eroded in the face of a U.S. adversary, who would then have greatly enhanced prospects of dominating a war termination process.

Third, the French speak of implementing proportional deterrence through a countervalue, as opposed to counterforce, strategy. It is a strategy aimed not at military forces, but at destruction of Soviet industrial centers and cities. In part, this strategy reflects the capabilities of French forces--they are limited in number and accuracy. And in part it reflects French preference to pursue a deterrence strategy that does not threaten Soviet strategic forces and thereby lead to a Soviet desire to preempt French forces in the event of crisis. The French want to have credible second-strike forces, not first-strike forces, to deter the Soviets from military adventurism in Europe. The nuclear-powered ballistic missile submarine (SSBN) has evolved as the most significant weapon system in this role.[5]

The language of French strategic doctrine is that of *dissuasion* (deterrence). The thrust of dissuasion for domestic purposes is to emphasize the defense of French territory as the purpose of nuclear weapons. Extensive public debate about the use of French nuclear weapons for any other purpose (such as the forward defense of West Germany) would intensify conflict over the political purposes to which French nuclear forces would be put and erode public support for French nuclear weapons policy.[6]

Since the mid-1970s, French leaders have backed away from the more extreme public positions taken earlier regarding the independence of their defense policy. In part, this retreat has entailed the restoration of some of the language of Alliance solidarity in French defense discourse. Former President Giscard d'Estaing identified France as a key player in the Alliance, and French nuclear weapons were said to be serving Alliance interests indirectly by serving French interests directly. Giscard d'Estaing also publicly questioned the salience of the "all or nothing" character of France's strategy for using nuclear weapons in a European war. He favored the development of a broader array of military options for France. The development of more flexibility inevitably entails greater inter-meshing of French security interests with Alliance interests.[7]

The Mitterrand administration has continued to search for more flexibility in serving France's security interests in Europe by means of greater public and private involvement in the Alliance. Mitterrand's decision to host the NATO ministerial meetings in Paris in June 1983 was of symbolic importance in this regard.[8] According to Pascal Krop of *Le Matin*, the Socialist government has pursued a double objective in reasserting France's commitment to the Alliance, namely, "to reassure the allies by assuring them of French support in case of conflict and, on the other hand, to develop a true European defense in case the Americans ultimately disengage themselves from Europe."[9]

In part, the language of Alliance solidarity is being restored to French defense discourse because of the perceived decline in Alliance cohesion. In theoretical terms, France's position is like that of an interest group as described in Mancur Olson's *The Logic of Collective Action*.[10] France could act with benign neglect when the United States, as the force shaping the Alliance, could by itself provide for the "public good" of collective defense. With a decline in the ability of the United States to do so, the public good of Western defense has eroded. The French are left in the position of remaining aloof and watching further deterioration in collective capabilities or contributing directly to the enhancement of Western defenses.[11] Increasingly, the French are finding that to deter the Soviets they must link their "independence" more directly and publicly with the efficacy of overall Western defense capabilities.

At the heart of French doctrinal problems is France's relationship with West Germany.[12] The development of closer Franco-German relations in the 1970s and 1980s has made the French more sensitive to the impact of the French nuclear issue on the Franco-German core of the European component of the Alliance.

The Giscard d'Estaing administration expanded the scope of potential interests served by French military power--including by implication the nuclear forces--by introducing the concept of an "enlarged sanctuary." The French have traditionally tied the use of nuclear weapons to the concept of the French territorial sanctuary. When the French chief of staff said publicly in 1976 that France was contemplating the defense of its European interests, specifically West Germany, as an "enlarged sanctuary," the implication was clear. The French government eased away from the use of this term when criticism was leveled that France was thereby slipping away from its traditional position of defending a national sanctuary, not an extended one.[13] The Mitterrand administration has, however, clearly identified the defense of West Germany as a "vital interest" for France.[14] The public commitment by West Germany and France to animate the security provisions of their 1963 comprehensive bilateral agreements entailed a provision for frequent meetings between the French and German ministries of defense.[15]

Clearly, French doctrine faces a central tension between the traditional emphasis on the primacy of independence, defined as protecting the national sanctuary with nuclear weapons, and the growing salience of the need to involve France in West German security issues.[16] In the context of justifying their exclusion from the U.S.-Soviet Intermediate-Range Nuclear Force (INF) Talks, the French have insisted that their nuclear weapons cannot be used to defend West Germany directly. But further development of a European alternative to U.S. dominance of the Alliance--which some French analysts favor--would require France to clearly identify their nuclear weapons with the defense of an enlarged sanctuary.

However, the French are now in the throes of tying their conventional forces more closely to the forward defense of West Germany.[17] Traditionally, they have identified their conventional forces in West Germany, supported by tactical nuclear weapons, with the function of "testing the enemy's intentions," or operating primarily as a tripwire for French strategic forces. With the formation of the rapid action force (FAR), the Mitterrand administration has underscored the importance of the forward defense of West Germany by conventional means. The decision by France and West Germany to co-produce a combat helicopter may signify the virtual commitment of the FAR to the forward defense concept.

In addition, when the Hades is deployed, probably in part with neutron warheads, it will be used to support the FAR and the First Army stationed in West Germany. As a result, French nuclear weapons will de facto become more closely linked to the forward defense of West Germany. But the French will stop short of making explicit public judgements about when or how their tactical nuclear weapons might or would be used in defending West Germany. France considers declaratory ambiguity on this question to be a key part of its deterrent posture.[18]

If NATO would not be able to mount a credible forward conventional defense, French doctrinal ambiguity is almost irrelevant to the militarily effective use of tactical nuclear weapons. It is questionable whether the Soviets would consider French use of tactical weapons as a realistic signal of a French intention to use strategic weapons, unless the tactical nuclear weapons were used in a militarily effective manner.

The French treatment of the tactical nuclear issue most clearly reveals the operation of several of the elements of French strategic thinking identified so far. When the French first deployed tactical nuclear weapons in the early 1970s, they indicated that these weapons were an inextricable part of the strategic deterrent. They were to function as the "last warning shot" to indicate French resolve to use strategic nuclear forces.[19] For the French, their tactical nuclear weapons are to be clearly distinguished from those of the United States. The French weapons are used as part of *dissuasion*, that is, to dissuade the Soviets from direct attacks against French territory. According to the French, their tactical nuclear weapons are not to be considered as battlefield weapons, whereas U.S. weapons are positioned to fight a limited nuclear war that might well engulf France. To maintain their limited role as a last warning shot to indicate French resolve, only a small number of French weapons need be deployed.

The basic French position on tactical nuclear weapons fits well into their national-sanctuary doctrine, but adapting to the Franco-German rapprochement has complicated the picture. First, Giscard d'Estaing publicly questioned the credibility of the "all or nothing" strategy. He suggested the need for a more flexible strategy, which implied a battlefield role for French tactical nuclear weapons.[20] Second, the decision in the mid-1970s to foster a research and development program for a neutron warhead fit in with a strategy for battlefield use of tactical nuclear weapons. The neutron warhead will be available in the mid-1980s but is not scheduled to be deployed before the Hades missile.[21] The neutron warhead can be used effectively primarily against Warsaw Pact armor, and its use is designed to involve follow-on attacks by conventional forces.[22] The deployment of the neutron warhead might then imply a willingness by France to engage in the forward defense of West Germany with a mix of conventional and tactical nuclear forces in a battlefield situation.[23]

Third, some French analysts have expressed concern that the quality of the last warning shot to be delivered against Soviet forces needs to be enhanced. There is a need to provide a real pause to Soviet military actions on the European battlefield to allow time for a favorable war termination process.[24] A forward defense of West Germany bolstered by· tactical nuclear weapons could force such a pause on the Soviets.

Tactical nuclear weapons are "counter-force" in character. The Soviets probably perceive French tactical nuclear weapons, especially the new-generation weapons, as significant factors affecting the success of their operations on the European battlefield. The tactical nuclear problem reflects a central tension in French doctrine between the public commitment to independence and the public commitment to West Germany and the Alliance. The French are having difficulty having it both ways. They would like to insist that their tactical nuclear weapons are only a fuse that would light the strategic arsenal, but the Soviets might well perceive them as battlefield weapons. In addition, the West Germans may insist that the new generation of French tactical nuclear weapons ought to contribute to collective defense, not just to the defense of French territory.[25]

External Challenges

The French face a number of challenges to the credibility of their nuclear deterrent in the 1980s and 1990s, challenges that underscore a basic dilemma in their doctrine. The growth of Soviet military power presents the most significant challenges. Many French military analysts believe that the Soviets have adopted the conventional war option as their basic option for fighting a war in Europe.[26] Some of these analysts further believe that the threat to use nuclear weapons against Soviet territory is sufficient to deter the Soviets from attempting to implement their conventional option. Others believe, as does General Etienne Copel, that nuclear weapons deter only nuclear weapons and that therefore the Soviet conventional threat cannot be dealt with solely by nuclear means.[27]

French military analysts tend to believe that the Soviets have a number of advantages that would allow them to prevail in a protracted war fought only with conventional forces. Most significant in this regard are Soviet proximity to the European theater, Soviet mobilizational capabilities, and the size and scope of Soviet military reserves in terms of both manpower and material. Although a conventional war would in all likelihood overwhelm Western Europe, the Alliance can legitimately aspire to dissuade the Soviets from believing that they could quickly win such a war. For example, the deployment of the FAR has been justified, in part, by the need to deal with Soviet development of operational maneuver groups (OMGs).[28]

Other French analysts emphasize that the Soviets would plan to conduct nuclear strikes from the onset of a war in Europe. According to one such analyst, "The most reasonable hypothesis (for the beginning of a war) would be that of a nuclear attack conducted with highly accurate ballistic missiles capable of destroying from a distance the adversary's means of combat, especially catching them by surprise."[29] This judgement is bolstered by assertions that Soviet doctrine is based on nuclear warfighting as the basic military option for a European conflict.[30]

Some French analysts are also concerned with the Soviets' growing capability to implement a "flanking option" against Western Europe.[31] Soviet power projection forces could be used to threaten vital lines of supply in a crisis, and nuclear forces would not necessarily be useful in deterring Soviet actions in this regard. Strong Western conventional forces, coupled with good military and diplomatic relations with Third World raw-material-supplying states (especially with the Arab Middle East), are critical to deterring the Soviets from attempting military flanking actions. But when French doctrine talks of deterrence, it is concerned primarily with the use of nuclear weapons in a massive strike against Soviet territory to deter Soviet military actions against France proper. The exercise of a flanking option by the Soviets against France by means of conventional forces outside Europe is not covered.

A number of technological developments by the Soviet military threaten the viability of French nuclear forces. First, the greater precision of Soviet nuclear warheads with lower yields (reducing collateral damage) provides the Soviets with an increasingly credible posture for conducting limited nuclear strikes against nuclear forces based in France.[32] The Soviets would then have reduced France to its sea-based deterrent, which might well allow them to dominate a war termination process with France.

Second, the growth in the capability of the Soviet air force--in both munitions and aircraft--provides the Soviets with the possibility of destroying with conventional ordnance all French land-based nuclear systems but the IRBMs.[33] What would be a credible French response to such a Soviet conventional strike?

Third, Soviet advances in antisubmarine warfare (ASW) might well undermine the credibility of the French sea-based deterrent. The heavy reliance by the French on the SSBN makes them especially concerned with the growth of the Soviet ASW threat. The French appear confident, however, that the SSBN will remain a viable second-strike deterrent for some time to come.[34]

Fourth, significant Soviet breakthroughs in ballistic missile defense (BMD) would call into question the ability of French ballistic missiles to penetrate Soviet defenses. Soviet BMD breakthroughs, coupled with advantages in passive defense and geographic expanse, could erode the political will of France to use nuclear weapons.[35] Why should France commit national suicide if it is only able to deliver a "slap in the face," and not a fatal blow, to the Soviets?

Fifth, the density and increasing quality of Soviet air defenses make it difficult for France to replace the ballistic missile with an air-delivered weapon as the main strategic weapon. The French could develop increasingly longer-range standoff missiles, but the more sophisticated guidance systems associated with U.S. air-launched cruise missiles (ALCMs) might well be beyond their technological grasp.[36]

The variety of technological possibilities for Soviet military developments threatens in various ways the core of French strategic doctrine—independence, proportional deterrence, and countervalue. Independence could be threatened by the growing need to cooperate with the United States or the United Kingdom in developing various aspects of strategic weapons technology. Proportional deterrence could be undercut by dramatic improvements in Soviet strategic defense capabilities against French systems, both before and after launch. The countervalue strategy, especially, could be undermined by a significant expansion of Soviet BMD.

The Soviets pose an arms control challenge as well as a military challenge to the French. The Soviet Union has insisted that French nuclear systems be explicitly recognized in the INF negotiations as a component of the Western deterrent. The French do not wish to recognize a broader role for their nuclear weapons than simply the defense of their "vital interests." Ironically, the Soviets are, in effect, pushing the French in the direction of playing a broader European role, although their intention is simply to undermine the French defense consensus.

The French position is challenged to a lesser extent by its allies, especially the United States and West Germany. The Americans challenge the French position in two major ways. First, the United States, in developing its own military (especially strategic) technology, stimulates Soviet deployments, which in turn are threatening to French systems.[37] If the Americans deploy BMD systems to protect their ICBMs, similar Soviet deployments would significantly undercut the credibility of the French deterrent. The development of U.S.

cruise missile technology has prompted the Soviets to improve their air defenses to such an extent that the air-delivered alternative for France is not an easy one by any means, especially when considered against enhanced Soviet conventional attack capabilities against the French air force.

Second, the development by the United States of new conventional weapon technologies could foster change in NATO doctrine.[38] Such changes might imply the transformation of the "forward defense of West Germany" into a campaign to conduct conventional interdiction missions into Eastern Europe. That kind of change in doctrine would seriously complicate French independence, especially with regard to defining the role of French tactical nuclear weapons as a warning shot.

The United States clearly would like France to play a greater role in the conventional defense of Europe. Although recognizing the significance of French nuclear weapons as an additional deterrent to the Soviet Union, Americans hope that France will augment its conventional forces and link them more directly with the defense of Europe. American and French interests coincide to the extent that France strengthens its ties to European defense (e.g., the FAR). To the extent that nuclear forces drain conventional forces, in terms of budgets and force structure, those interests diverge.

The West Germans also challenge the French position in several ways. First, some politicians in West Germany have indicated that France should in some way include its strategic forces in the INF arms control process. The Social Democratic Party officially adopted such a position at its conferences in 1982 and 1983. Some members of the ruling coalition are also sympathetic to this position. For example, Juergen Todenhoeger, arms policy spokesman for the ruling alliance of Christian Democrats and the Christian Social Union, called for a merger of U.S., French, and British nuclear forces in European arms control talks.[39]

Second, West German officials want France to contribute more fully and publicly to the forward defense of Germany with conventional forces.[40] These officials have been concerned that the current French economic downturn and commitment to nuclear modernization will lead to a reduction in French conventional capabilities. Consequently, West Germany might well try to use the formation of the FAR as an opportunity to deepen French commitment to long-term conventional modernization.

Third, West Germany will continue to press France to clarify the role of its tactical nuclear weapons. West Germany has always been understandably uneasy with the notion that French tactical nuclear weapons are to be used simply as a last warning shot to indicate French resolve to use strategic nuclear weapons. West Germany is concerned lest this French last warning shot provoke a Soviet nuclear reprisal against NATO forces on German territory.

The German and French governments have established a new institutional mechanism for conducting discussions of joint security issues.[41] In October 1982, the German and French defense ministries agreed to form a joint Defense Committee. There are three working groups, one each for political and strategic questions, military cooperation, and armaments cooperation. These working groups meet two to three times a year. In addition, there are regular talks between the German and French general staffs.

The focus of the current dialogue between France and Germany has been primarily on the need to expand joint arms procurement decisions.[42] Most recently, the discussion has focused on the joint development of a combat helicopter. The two governments have agreed to build 400 of these helicopters and to plan joint development of a fighter plane for the 1990s.

Discussions have also been held on the relationship between French and German conventional forces. For example, there has been extensive consultation with the Germans over the development of the French FAR and its deployment in West Germany in times of crisis. There has also been talk about the tactical nuclear problem, but reports on this discussion are contradictory. The French have apparently provided more detailed information on the development and possible use of their tactical nuclear force. In particular, they are said to have shared their current thinking about the new generation of tactical nuclear weapons. But to date France has not indicated any willingness to allow the Germans a participatory role in the use of these weapons. According to a high-ranking German official, "We want some sort of nuclear guarantee whereby France regards German territory, East and West, as its [Bonn's] own security area."[43]

Despite such instances of increased cooperation, there is a central tension at the heart of the Franco-German dialogue. For the Germans, only the U.S. nuclear forces provide the ultimate deterrent to Soviet forces in Europe. The French can play but a subordinate role, although France and Germany could play a more significant supplemental role in the Alliance (especially in terms of cooperation in conventional military forces). In contrast, for the French, the dialogue with the Germans is at the heart of any Europeanization of the Alliance.[44] France seeks a central role for Europe within the Alliance, not a revitalization of U.S. leadership over Europe. It will be difficult to resolve the basic tension between the objectives of Germany (to strengthen French ties to the U.S.-led Alliance) and of France (to strengthen the power of the European component of the Alliance).

The Dilemma and Its Resolution

The basic political purpose of French nuclear forces is to ensure French independence. The difficulty is that the growth in Soviet global military capabilities, the decline in Alliance cohesion, and the increased importance of West Germany to French security all call into question the meaning of independence if it is limited to the defense of French territory or of a narrowly construed definition of France's "vital interests."

The growth in Soviet military capabilities undercuts the credibility of a French "all or nothing" strategy. The Soviets might try to degrade French nuclear forces gradually through conventional means. The Soviets might attempt selective destruction of French nuclear forces-- the prosecution of SSBNs at sea, air strikes against the French air force, and commando raids against the IRBMs. For example, Captain John Hyland has characterized the Soviet antisubmarine warfare (ASW) threat to French SSBNs as follows:

> The expansion of the Soviet Navy's ASW capability in quantity and quality of aircraft, surface ships, and submarines has created the numbers of platforms and the technical capacity to locate and to track continuously a strategic submarine force of France's size. No major advance or breakthrough in ASW technology would be needed. Whether or not the USSR would attempt to locate and track all deployed French SSBNs is a matter of conjecture. The Soviet Navy's capacity to execute the mission is not. And the French Navy's emphasis on the SSBN protection mission reflects, in part, a concern for this possible scenario.[45]

What would be the appropriate French response to selective and gradual destruction of its nuclear forces by Soviet conventional forces?

The second complicating trend, the decline in Alliance cohesion, increases the salience of the French role in the Alliance. If France fails to commit its nuclear assets to a European role, it can play that role only with its conventional forces. But if France starves conventional forces to feed nuclear ones, it will weaken intra-Alliance relations rather than strengthen them.

Implementation of an "enlarged sanctuary" doctrine, however, might erode the French defense consensus.[46] Although there is broad support for French nuclear policy, this support does not extend to the notion of an enlarged sanctuary. As a result, French policy-makers are unable to confront directly the broader European concerns generated by the modernization of French nuclear forces. Hence, a central dilemma for French policy-makers is posed by the contradiction between the need, induced by external pressures, to expand the concept of independence, and the need to maintain the myth that French territory is "sanctuarized" by the possession of nuclear weapons, this myth being central to the domestic defense consensus.

How might France best resolve the dilemma or tension between "independence" and "European security"? The French defense debate of the early 1980s has provided three major alternative responses to this difficult problem. First, France could "resolve" this tension by ignoring it. France would continue to emphasize the centrality of its nuclear forces to the defense of France proper. To the extent France made a contribution to European security, it would be by indirectly supplementing the U.S. nuclear "guarantee" by serving as an alternative decision-making center for nuclear reprisals against any Soviet attack directed at France, especially a nuclear one. To the extent that the Soviets could not conceive of fighting a war in the European theater without invading France, the "sanctuarization" of France by nuclear weapons contributes to deterrence on the European level.

There are maximalist and minimalist versions of this position. The maximalist version, espoused by some Gaullists, advocates a significant increase in the French strategic arsenal. The Gaullist party, the Rassemblement pour la République (RPR), proposed an alternative Military Program Law for 1984-1988, in which nine SSBNs would be operational by 1994.[47] It is difficult to see how such a buildup could be funded without significant cuts in French conventional forces. The maximalist position frequently carries with it a belief in the nonutility of conventional forces in deterring the Soviets. The adversary is painted as planning a nuclear campaign against Europe, from which France could protect itself only by possessing a secure second-strike strategic force.

The notion that strategic nuclear weapons "sanctuarize" France implies that West Germany must fend for itself. Some Gaullists have stated to the author that they would rather see West Germany occupied than fire a single nuclear weapon in its defense. As one Gaullist posed the question to the author, "Why should France commit national suicide to defend West Germany?" Another Gaullist pointed out that West Germany's "fending for itself" could not include the acquisition of nuclear weapons. This person would rather see Germany "Finlandized" than equipped with an independent nuclear deterrent.

The minimalist position is the one espoused by the Parti Communiste Français (PCF). As a member of the governing coalition until July 1984, the PCF nominally agreed with the Parti Socialiste Français (PSF) on the "essentials" of French security policy. But the agreement on "essentials" did not carry over to the "details" of concrete policy, for the PCF has only supported a limited nuclear modernization as the core of French defense policy.[48] By starving conventional forces, the nuclear program reduces the power of the uniformed military, most notably the ground forces. Past struggles between the Left and the army have not been forgotten by many members of the PCF. Paradoxically, the PCF supports the nuclear policy as a way of reducing "militarism" in French society, rather than increasing it.[49]

A variant of the minimalist version of "independence" has been espoused by some members of the left wing of the PSF, notably the CERES (Centre d'Etudes, de Recherches, et d'Education Socialiste) group. For this group, the advantage of an independent nuclear deterrent for France is to allow France to avoid an "entangling" alliance with the unreliable and erratic Americans. Also, by having an independent deterrent, France does not have to "overcommit" resources to the military sector.

Both the maximalist and minimalist versions of independence would make no change in French doctrine. The political purpose of French nuclear forces would be identified as solely the protection of French territory. The strength of this position is the preservation of the historical consensus that has emerged in France regarding nuclear weapons. Its weakness is the absence of any response to the erosion of the "public good" of Western defense. Although rational from the standpoint of French domestic considerations, such a position of independence would appear irresponsible to other members of the Western Alliance in the challenging European security environment of the 1980s and 1990s.

The second alternative calls for France to "resolve" the tension not by changing doctrine, but by augmenting its ability to participate in the forward defense of Germany by conventional means. Nuclear weapons would be used to protect French territory primarily, and French "vital interests" secondarily. Ambiguity would surround exactly what is covered by the concept of vital interests.

The current positions of the Mitterrand administration embody this alternative.[50] French doctrine has clearly not changed under Mitterrand. The administration has ritualistically asserted that French doctrine has not been modified, in part to allow changes in French military capability to unfold without a debilitating doctrinal debate, that is, a debate about the political implications of changing French military policy. The administration has used the concept of vital interests to cloak in ambiguity the political uses of French nuclear forces, especially tactical nuclear weapons.

The major alteration that the Mitterrand administration has introduced in French forces is the rapid action force (FAR). It is clear that the creation of this force has been motivated by political objectives, the most significant, to enhance Franco-German security cooperation.[51] Defense Minister Hernu and the newly appointed commander of the FAR have gone so far as to identify the role of this force as having the capability to participate in the forward defense of Germany. This role would require close cooperation with NATO in peacetime as well as wartime.[52]

Within France the new FAR has stimulated much discussion. The government has been severely criticized for the changes in French doctrine that the deployment of the FAR seems to imply. The author witnessed the all-night debate of 2 December 1983 in the French Senate on the defense budget. Several members of the opposition prominently displayed the newspaper article by the FAR commander suggesting a NATO role for this force. The mere suggestion of such a role carries with it an air of illegitimacy to many French citizens.

The government has responded vigorously to the charge that the deployment of the FAR changes French doctrine. The government claims that it is only creating more flexible deterrent options.[53] Part of the force will be deployed in the south of France and would have to be moved northward to play its role. One government spokesman claims that such movement would provide an important "signal" to the Soviets of French intentions in a prewar setting, thereby adding to the range of French deterrent options.[54]

The strength of this second option--independence plus participation in the forward conventional defense of West Germany--is its practical emphasis on altering capabilities. The Mitterrand administration may well have set the objective of accelerating a process of security cooperation with West Germany, which will then have a political logic of its own in 10 to 15 years.

In other words, rather than debating the difficult problem of whether French nuclear weapons will ever be able to provide extended deterrence for West Germany, why not focus on the practical dimensions of expanding Franco-German cooperation? The weakness of this position is that without doctrinal change, at some point it will not be clear to either the French public or France's allies that France is serious about a European role for its military forces. If France continues to value its nuclear forces far more than its conventional forces, the absence of some form of commitment of those nuclear forces to West Germany casts doubt on the sincerity of France's intention to play a European role.

Nonetheless, the Mitterrand administration is clearly modifying the French concept of independence in defense policy. As a high-ranking French official noted in 1983, "It is often said that 'The policy of France is independent.' It would be better to say: 'The policy of France is as independent as possible.' Absolute independence does not exist any more in the realm of security than it does in the realm of economics."[55]

A variant of the second alternative would go further and make explicit the doctrinal changes necessary to identify French conventional forces with the forward defense of Germany and with other Alliance military missions. The political coalition of former President Giscard d'Estaing, the Union pour la Démocratie Française (UDF), has clearly asserted the need for France to express its solidarity with the Alliance.[56] The UDF has criticized the Mitterrand administration for overinvesting in nuclear forces. "The decision to give increased priority to nuclear arms, according to the government's own statements, in a reduced budget package is likely to produce a purely illusory 'sanctuarization' of defense whose inevitable result is neutralism in Europe and impotence in the world."[57] The secretary-general of the UDF even went so far as to speak of the French nuclear force as "a new Maginot line." Michel Pinton meant that nuclear forces are also "self-deterring" and France needs strong conventional forces augmented by cooperation with the forces of the Alliance to protect French security interests.[58] Needless to say, there was a vigorous negative public reaction to Pinton's turn of phrase, which, in part, led to his resignation.

A well-known advocate of greater cooperation with the Alliance in conventional forces, François de Rose, has articulated the problem of independence as follows: "It has often been said that France has a policy of independent defense. It would be more appropriate to say that France has an independent defense policy. The confusion is revealing, for an independent defense policy does not absolutely bar us from cooperating with our allies for common defense whereas an independent defense links it to neutrality."[59] Such a shift in the public characterization of the French defense effort is clearly required for a process of deepened cooperation with the Alliance.

Under the third alternative, France could assign her independent nuclear force a more ambitious role than simply deterring Soviet attacks against French territory. Several augmentations of the role of French nuclear weapons have been suggested in recent years--the deployment of a large nuclear force armed with neutron warheads for battlefield use, the extension of some form of nuclear guarantee to West Germany, and the indirect or direct creation of some form of European nuclear force stimulated by French example and/or effort.

Some analysts have suggested that France ought to equip its ground forces with significantly upgraded nuclear firepower. The most frequently discussed candidate for this role has been the neutron warhead.[60] If French forces were armed with neutron weapons, they would become a much more formidable barrier to any Soviet armored assault into Europe. By being prepared to take the nuclear battle to Soviet forces in the European theater, France would significantly enhance deterrence of Soviet "limited" war options. The mere existence of an anti-cities French nuclear capability is not enough to deter the Soviets from attempting to realize "limited" war aims.

Diverse voices in France have suggested the possibility of extending some form of nuclear guarantee to West Germany. At the heart of such a guarantee is the question of the use of French tactical nuclear weapons.[61] Almost always the guarantee in question would be designed to supplement, not supplant, the U.S. nuclear guarantee. For example, Michel Tatu of *Le Monde* has argued that when the new Hades missile is ready for deployment, it could be placed on German soil under a dual-key arrangement.[62] Also, in a speech delivered in Bonn, Jacques Chirac, mayor of Paris and leader of the Gaullist party, argued that French nuclear forces should be involved in some form of a European guarantee to West German security.[63]

Several variants of the idea of a European nuclear force have been aired recently by French analysts.[64] One variant emphasizes the importance for European defense of the simultaneous modernization of the French and British forces. The very fact that both forces will be augmented in the 1980s and 1990s enhances the nuclear protection of Europe.[65] A second variant would go further and encourage direct British-French nuclear cooperation, in joint development of their strategic forces or of a tactical nuclear force for Germany. One French analyst suggested to the author that a joint French-British cruise missile force could be developed to provide a "nuclear cover" for French and British forces in West Germany. A third variant is much more ambitious and would seek to proliferate nuclear warheads among the major West European states, including West Germany.[66] This variant rests on the assumption that deterrence would be enhanced if the Soviets faced a multitude of nuclear decision-making centers. This variant would require, among other things, abrogating the Nuclear Nonproliferation Treaty and confronting the politically explosive issue of the possession of nuclear weapons by the West Germans. In light of the various options to "resolve" the problem of defining the role of French nuclear weapons for West European defense (table 4.1), what are the probable scenarios for the evolution of French defense policy and doctrine in the 1980s and 1990s? Most likely is the continued highest priority accorded nuclear weapons with no doctrinal change that would give French nuclear weapons a direct role in European defense. Precisely because of serious disagreement over doctrinal change, it is unlikely that such change will occur, but the absence of change in doctrine does not foreclose changes in capability. For example, the accretion of French strategic power may foreshadow the modification of French countervalue doctrine to encompass some counterforce options.

Two debates over the development of the French nuclear force structure have a reasonable probability of occurring. The first debate would involve questioning the wisdom of placing too many of France's nuclear eggs in the ballistic missile basket. In light of perceived impending BMD deployments by the superpowers, no prudent French strategic planner can afford not to develop a serious alternative to the ballistic missile. Especially significant might be the development of a sea-launched cruise missile program. The second debate would revolve around tactical nuclear weapons. Some might wish to reduce the tactical component of the nuclear arsenal in order to augment the strategic component. Others might wish to "nuclearize" either the FAR or First Army by giving it a neutron warhead battlefield system. Others might wish to change the mix of tactical nuclear systems in favor of either the Hades or the ASMP (short-range attack missile).

The second most likely scenario is for a process of Franco-German military cooperation in conventional forces to unfold in the 1980s, which would allow modifications in French doctrine to include Germany directly in the French security concept. The most likely area where France would provide a supplemental nuclear guarantee for Germany would involve the tactical nuclear force. Either some nuclear systems could be stationed directly on German soil or the French government could indicate its willingness to use tactical nuclear weapons based on French soil in the forward defense of Germany.

The least likely scenario is that France would reemphasize conventional forces at the expense of nuclear forces. Some increased cooperation is possible, but it will stop short of France's rejoining the integrated NATO command, such an action being beyond the pale in French politics.

In short, the modernization of its nuclear forces will continue to be the central priority for France. French nuclear weapons will most likely remain identified with the defense of French territory, but there

TABLE 4.1
FRENCH DEFENSE OPTIONS

Basic Option	Variants	Military or Security Locus
Asset primacy of independent nuclear deterrent	Maximalist	SSBN force augmented
	Minimalist	Modest nuclear force modernization
Independent nuclear deterrent plus forward defense of FRG by conventional forces	Franco-German cooperation	Nuclear modernization plus deployment of FAR
	Enhanced direct and public involvement by French conventional forces in NATO missions	Greater emphasis on enhancing NATO's conventional deterrent
Independent nuclear deterrent plus	Enhanced tactical nuclear "battlefield" capability	Neutron weapon
	Supplemental nuclear guarantee for FRG	Double-key system or Enlarged sanctuary
	"European" nuclear force	Indirect supplement or Active Franco-British cooperation or Nuclear proliferation within Western Europe

is increasing external pressure to define a broader role for them. The internal debate on the legitimacy of providing a broader role for French nuclear weapons might just succeed in creating a "moving consensus" in favor of incorporating West Germany in the French security concept. But strong domestic pressures impede the evolution of such a consensus, making it difficult for France to resolve its basic strategic dilemma.

Notes

1. For an interesting recent discussion of the impact of nuclear weapons on alliance politics, see Charles Zorgbide, *Les Alliances dans le système mondial* (Paris: PUF, 1983), chap. 9.

2. For a discussion of the development of French doctrine, see "La Défense," in *L'Etat et les citoyens,* vol. 5 (Paris: Commission du bilan de la France, 1982), 46-55. See also Jean Klein, "La Stratégie nucléaire de la France et les hypothèses de guerre en France," *Défense et sécurité,* vol. 5, 1982, 233-262.

3. See Lucien Poirier, *Des Stratégies nucléaires* (Paris: Hachette, 1977), chap. 15.

4. See Lucien Poirier, *Essais de stratégie théorique* (Paris: Strategique, 1982), 287-311.

5. See Pierre Lacoste, *Stratégie navale* (Paris: Fernand Nathan, 1981), 294.

6. See Dominique Moisi, "Les Limites du consensus," in *Pacifisme et dissuasion,* ed. Pierre Lellouche (Paris: Economica, 1983), 253-266.

7. See the various policy declarations of the Giscard d'Estaing administration contained in *Une Politique de défense pour la France* (Paris: Government print, 1981).

8. See *Washington Post,* 10 June 1983; *New York Times,* 9 June 1983.

9. Pascal Krop, *Les Socialistes et l'armée* (Paris: PUF, 1983), 148.

10. Mancur Olson, *The Logic of Collective Action* (Cambridge, Mass.: Harvard University Press, 1965).

11. This idea was suggested to me by Robert Gelbard of the United States Department of State and is acknowledged with his permission.

12. On Franco-German military cooperation, see Walter Schutze, "La Coopération franco-allemande dans le domaine militaire," in *Allemagnes d'aujourd'hui,* no. 84 (1984).

13. See Michael M. Harrison, *The Reluctant Ally: France and Atlantic Security* (Baltimore: Johns Hopkins University Press, 1981), 193-204.

14. Gen. Lacaze, "Politique de défense et stratégie militaire de la France," *Défense nationale,* June 1983, 16.

15. *FBIS Daily Report: Western Europe,* 22 October 1982, J-2.

16. See Joseph Rovan, "Bonn," *Politique internationale,* Spring 1982, 43- 66.

17. *Le Monde,* 1 June and 18 June 1983.

18. On the importance of declaratory ambiguity to disuassion, see Dominique David, "L'Alliance: notre arche et son déluge," *Stratégique,* no. 16 (1982): 83.

19. *Livre blanc sur la défense nationale* (Paris: Government print, 1972).

20. This has been most clearly stated by Giscard d'Estaing's political party, the Union pour la Démocratie Française, in *Une Doctrine de défense pour la France* (Paris: UDF, May 1980).

21. *FBIS Daily Report: Western Europe,* 28 June 1983, K-1.

22. See Maurice Leman, "Les Neutrons: l'arme anti-invasion pour une défense européenne," *Politique étrangère*, 1981, no. 2: 409-426.

23. Pascal Krop, *Le Matin*, 13 March 1982.

24. *Le Point*, 30 November 1981, 58-65.

25. *Der Speigel*, 18 October 1982, 31-32.

26. See, for example, the report by Senator M. Jacques Chaumont entitled *Défense: forces terrestres* (Paris: Sénat, 21 November 1983).

27. Etienne Copel, *Vaincre la guerre* (Paris: Editions Lieu Commun, 1984).

28. *Libération*, 18-19 June 1983.

29. Charles Zorgbide, *Le Risque de guerre* (Paris: PUF, 1981), 91.

30. See Henri Paris, *Stratégies soviétique et américaine* (Paris: Stratégique, 1980), 69.

31. See Jean-Paul Pigasse, *Le Bouclier d'Europe* (Paris: Seghers, 1982), 57.

32. See Gen. Gallois, "L'Option zéro est inacceptable pour l'Europe," *Géopolitique*, April 1983, 104-112. Gallois has elaborated his argument in "Precision, the Fourth Age of Strategy," unpublished paper, November 1983. Also see Gallois and John Train, "When a Nuclear Strike is Thinkable," *Wall Street Journal*, 22 March 1984.

33. On the problem of the threat posed to France by the Soviet Air Force see the report by M. Albert Voilquin entitled *Les Moyens de la défense aérienne* (Paris: Sénat, 20 April 1983).

34. See Hubert Moineville, *La Guerre navale* (Paris: PUF, 1982), 54-55.

35. Jean Ducret in *Armée nouvelle*, 1983, no. 9:10-11.

36. See Lawrence Freedman, "The European Nuclear Powers: Britain and France," in *Cruise Missiles*, ed. Richard K. Betts (Washington, D.C.: Brookings Institution, 1981), 464-476.

37. See articles by Jean-Paul Pigasse, *Défense et securité*, 20 April, 28 April, and 1 May 1983.

38. The tension between changing American doctrine and the traditional French position on defense is evident in *Defense and Arms Control Policies in the 1980s*, Triangle Paper no. 26 (New York: Trilateral Commission, 1983), 66-67, 90, 103-104. On changing American doctrine and its possible impact on France, see *La Nouvelle Doctrine de guerre américaine et la securité de l'Europe*, Cahiers d'études stratégiques no. 1 (Paris: Centre Interdisciplinaire de Recherches sur la Paix et d'Etudes Stratégiques, 1983).

39. *Washington Post*, 18 April 1984.

40. See Konrad Seitz, "La Coopération franco-allemande dans le domaine de la politique de securité," *Politique étrangère*, 1982, no. 4:979-987.

41. Wolfgang Flume, "Weapons Development With France," *Wehrtechnik*, February 1984, 25.

42. On the general significance of European armaments production to the Mitterrand administration, see the speech by Defense Minister Hernu delivered to the West European Assembly, 1 December 1983, unpublished draft text obtained from the French Ministry of Defense.

43. *Washington Post*, 20 April 1984.

44. See Bernard Adrien [pseud.], "La France et les interrogations allemandes," *Politique étrangère*, 1982, no. 4:967-977.

45. Capt. John J. Hyland, "French Nuclear Forces," *Naval War College Review*, forthcoming.

46. On the fragility of the French defense consensus, see Pierre Lellouche, "France and the Euromissiles," *Foreign Affairs*, no. 62 (Winter 1983-84): 318-334.

47. *Contre-Projet de loi de programmation militaire, 1984-1988* (Paris: RPR, 1983).

48. On the PCF's nuclear policy, see Nicole Gnesotto, "Le PCF et les euromissiles," *Politique étrangère*, 1983, no.3:701-711.

49. On the relationship between the PCF and the military, see Yves Roucaute, *Le PCF et l'armée* (Paris: PUF, 1983).

50. For an interesting statement of the administration's position by an informal participant, see Jacques Huntzinger, "Défense de la France, securité de l'Europe," *Politique étrangère*, 1983, no. 2:395-402.

51. See the column by Rowland Evans and Robert Novak, "Mitterrand Looks to Germany," *Washington Post*, 16 December 1983.

52. See Olivier Wormser, "Quelle politique de défense?" *L'Express*, 9-15 December 1983, 25.

53. See the arguments by Hernu in *Le Monde*, 25 October 1983.

54. François Cailleteau, "La Force d'action rapide," *Etudes polémologiques*, bulletin no. 3, 1983, 5.

55. As quoted by Dominique de Montvalon, "France-Otan: la fin des soupçons," *L'Express*, 10-16 June 1983, 94.

56. *Une Doctrine de défense pour la France; La Loi de programmation militaire nécessaire à la France en 1983* (Paris: UDF, April 1983); *Défendre l'Europe* (Paris: UDF, March 1984).

57. *Le Monde*, 20 April 1983.

58. *Le Monde*, 16 June 1983.

59. François de Rose, "La Défense de la France et de l'Europe," *Défense nationale*, December 1982, 73. See also de Rose's book, *Contre la stratégie des Curiaces* (Paris: Julliard, 1983).

60. The best-known proponent of this idea is Marc Geneste. See Samuel T. Cohn and Marc Geneste, *Echec à la guerre: La bombe à neutrons* (Paris: Editions Copernic, 1980); Marc Geneste, "Why the Allies Need the Neutron Bomb," *Wall Street Journal*, 17 August 1983.

61. See Pierre Eylau-Wagram [pseud.], "Propositions pour une stratégie française de 1980 à 1990," *Politique étrangère*, 1981, no. 1:121-136.

62. *Le Monde*, 4-5 December 1983.

63. *Le Monde*, 28 October 1983.

64. For an overview of this problem, see Jean Klein, "Mythes et réalités de la défense de l'Europe," *Politique étrangère*, 1983, no. 2: 315-336. Also see *Le Nouvel Observateur*, 2 December 1983.

65. See the interview with Gen. Gallois in *Libération*, 19 October 1983.

66. See Michel Manel, *L'Europe sans défense* (Paris: Berger-Levrault, 1982). This book was reissued in 1983 under a new title, *L'Europe face aux SS-20*.

5
Soviet Perspectives on French Security Policy

This chapter provides an overview of Soviet analysts' perceptions of French security policy since the establishment of the independent nuclear force in the mid-1960s.[1] The examination of Soviet perceptions is divided into three sections. In the first section, the evolution of French security policy as perceived by Soviet analysts is outlined. Soviet analysts argue that the original policy of General de Gaulle of independence has been progressively modified. The French are perceived to be trying to bolster the West European component of the Alliance in order to strengthen the Alliance.

In the second section, Soviet perceptions of the French force structure are analyzed to determine Soviet views on the independence of French forces. Soviet analysts tend to argue that French nuclear forces are, by and large, operationally independent of other Western forces. Politically, however, they are considered to be an integral component of the Western Alliance's nuclear potential. In contrast, French conventional forces are considered to be integral elements of NATO's military potential in Europe, both operationally and politically, regardless of French pretentions of independence. Prudent Soviet military planners would clearly plan to operate against French conventional forces in time of war. There is, however, some disagreement in the Soviet literature over when France would use its nuclear forces. Some think France would use nuclear forces solely to defend French territory; others believe French nuclear forces would be used before French territory was invaded. Prudent Soviet military planners would undoubtedly plan, at a minimum, to conduct conventional military operations against French nuclear forces, on land as well as at sea.

In the third section, Soviet perceptions of the political and military impact of French security policy are analyzed. It is clear that Soviet analysts are more concerned with the political impact of French security policy (including the French nuclear forces) than with the strictly military repercussions. The major political impact of concern to the Soviets is the encouragement France has given to the emergence and growth of an independent West European "power center." Although France's challenge to American "hegemony" in Western Europe is significant to Soviet calculations about American power, it is France's contribution to the West European "power center" that worries the Russians more.

The Soviet literature on France is of relatively high quality and reflects a serious effort to comprehend the structure and dynamics of French policy. Soviet analysis of France has not been excessively shackled by an "official" view of French reality. When Soviet policymakers do not repress analysis by imposing an official view, the quality and vigor of the Soviet analytical effort are often impressive. Such is the case with the literature under review.

The specialized literature, however, does operate within broad limits set by established policy. In the 1970s the official commitment to detente meant that the Soviet specialist on France was obligated to demonstrate some relationship between the thrust of French policy and the "favorable" atmosphere of detente. In the 1980s, especially in 1983 and 1984, the official emphasis on the inclusion of French nuclear forces in the Intermediate-Range Nuclear Force (INF) talks meant that the Soviet French analyst was obliged to demonstrate how France contributed to the Western Alliance's nuclear potential or policy as a whole.

The views summarized in this chapter are those of Soviet French specialists who work in various foreign policy "think tanks" and diplomatic and military institutions. When views of specialists are printed in the major Soviet newspapers, notably *Pravda* or *Izvestiia*, these views have been designated especially authoritative by the Soviet leadership. It is often the case that commentary by Soviet specialists on military and foreign policy anticipates or shapes the official position. For example, the recent Soviet diplomatic protest against the West European Union's lifting of remaining restrictions on the joint production of arms with the Federal Republic of Germany was framed in the same language used by Soviet specialists months before.

The Soviet perspectives reconstructed in this chapter are influential in shaping or expressing official Soviet opinion.

Nonetheless, Soviet decisions affecting French security may well not reflect these opinions if high-ranking Soviet decision-makers choose to ignore them. Thus, the perspectives presented here are the views of Soviet specialists on France on the scope, nature, and dynamics of French security policy and are an expression of the specialized opinion informing Soviet decisions affecting policy toward France.

The Evolution of French Security Policy

Soviet analysts perceive that French security policy has gone through three phases of development since France created its independent nuclear force. The first phase (the 1960s) was the establishment of the French policy of independence associated with Charles de Gaulle. The second phase (the 1970s) was the adjustment of the original Gaullist system, especially by President Giscard d'Estaing in the mid-1970s, to better accommodate West European and American interests. The third phase (the 1980s) has seen an acceleration of the processes of the 1970s. President François Mitterrand has more fully embraced West European security interests and has promoted a partial return to Atlanticism.

President de Gaulle (1958-1969)

General de Gaulle sought to create a security policy for France that would give greater independence than had been provided by the Fourth Republic's close ties with the Americans in the NATO Alliance. De Gaulle tried unsuccessfully to reorganize the Alliance to give France a bigger role in Western decision-making. As a result of this failure, de Gaulle made the decision to withdraw French forces from the integrated military command dominated by the United States. As B. Khalosha wrote in 1966, "France's present policy in NATO [the withdrawal from the integrated command] is not the reason for the crisis in the bloc, but rather a natural consequence [of American diktat]."[2] For Soviet analysts, the sine qua non of French independence was and remains the withdrawal from NATO's integrated military command. As V. Baranovskii noted, President de Gaulle's "strategy of 'defense against all azimuths' and the establishment of a certain distance from its ally across the ocean favorably affected France's international status because with this not only were the French armed forces withdrawn from the American-NATO command, but the potential for the country to be automatically drawn into a war also decreased."[3]

Soviet analysts hoped that France's withdrawal from NATO's integrated command would be the beginning of the end for the Alliance.[4] Although such hopes were short-lived, the political and symbolic impact of the French action has not been. I. A. Koloskov noted in 1976 in his book on the Fifth Republic's foreign policy, "The withdrawal of France from NATO's integrated military system weakened the Atlantic Alliance. The example of France could not help but exercise an important influence on other European members of the Alliance in strengthening their opposition to American hegemony in Europe and other regions."[5]

The symbolism of President de Gaulle's "anti-American" actions has had a deep influence on Soviet analysts, inducing them to look largely with favor on him and his historical legacy. Evidence of this esteem is seen in the tone and substance of the 500-page official Soviet biography of de Gaulle, which has gone through two editions, the second issued in 74,000 copies.[6]

President de Gaulle not only distanced himself from the United States, but also began to develop a "special relationship" with the Soviet Union. According to N. Komin, "At certain historical stages de Gaulle paid tribute to anti-Sovietism, but there is no doubt that it was realism in his attitude towards the Soviet Union, especially in the last years of his activity as President of the Republic...that clearly prevailed. De Gaulle's concept of 'cooperation between France and Russia' remained true, to a greater or lesser extent, his whole life."[7] De Gaulle is seen by Soviet analysts to have promoted Soviet-French cooperation in economic, diplomatic, and political affairs. His motivation was to enhance the prestige of France as a world power.[8]

The linkage between France's "anti-Americanism" and detente with the Soviet Union was clearly made by V.A. Zorin, the Soviet Ambassador to Paris from 1965 to 1971. Writing in 1983, he noted the following:

> Early 1966 saw the announcement of a forthcoming official visit of the President of the French Republic General de Gaulle to the USSR. It was a dramatic indication of the favourable course of Soviet-French relations and detente.
>
> By the time of his visit to the USSR de Gaulle had taken a number of major steps that to a certain degree made France free of foreign dependence, primarily on the USA and the U.S.-led NATO military-political alliance. The steps were taken after repeated and unsuccessful attempts to reach agreement with the USA on France's equal participation in the control of the organization (by means of creating a triumvirate of the USA, Britain, and France which would make decisions on key matters of NATO's foreign policy orientation and the use of nuclear weapons) and on the conduct of its policy on the basis of a realistic

assessment of the world balance of forces and the role of the USSR and the rest of
the socialist system in international relations in the nuclear age.

It was obvious to de Gaulle, and he said as much in his *Mémoires d'Espoir*
published in 1970, that the Soviet Union's possession of high-yield nuclear
missiles threw new light on the U.S. might and its capacity to defend Europe in
case of war, and that NATO was no longer in a position effectively to guarantee
the security of France.[9]

A significant implication of de Gaulle's belief that NATO could no
longer effectively guarantee the security of France was the need to
have an independent nuclear force.[10] The French nuclear force was
declared to be designed to deal with "threats" from all directions,
although the Soviets knew full well against whom it was directed.
Nonetheless, the main purpose of the French nuclear force was
political, not military; it was seen to be needed to create a political
"space" for independence. As was noted in a 1963 article, "In de
Gaulle's plans the atomic bomb is not just a weapon in the arsenal for
war against the Soviet Union, but also *an instrument of blackmail
with regard to the 'allies' of French imperialism.*"[11] In a 1965 article, it
was asserted that France was trying to use its nuclear forces as a
"trump card in the political card game" with its "allies."[12]

Nonetheless, Soviet analysts did note that France maintained her
treaty commitments to the Atlantic Alliance and continued to rely on
American involvement in West European defense. The end result was
the creation of an additional threat to the Soviet Union. As A. E.
Efremov noted in his major book on NATO nuclear weapons
(published in 1972), "the danger of these theories [of French nuclear
strategists] was already distinctly apparent from the fact that the
French military theoreticians emphasized that a small nuclear power
can play the role of a 'detonator' or a 'catalyst,' and by its actions,
contribute to drawing a powerful nuclear ally into the war...."[13]

One element of de Gaulle's foreign policy was of particular concern
to the Soviets: the aspiration to build a powerful Western Europe. The
Soviets, like de Gaulle, have been skeptical of Europe's ability to
develop transnationally through an organization like the European
Economic Community (EEC). De Gaulle's desired path to strengthen
Western Europe was to establish a directorate of the major West
European powers. Although at the time of de Gaulle's presidency
French actions increased tensions among West Europeans, Soviet
analysts continued to be concerned with the long-term potential for
France to stimulate West European cooperation.[14]

President Pompidou (1969-1974)

De Gaulle's immediate successor, Georges Pompidou, was perceived to have gained ascendency primarily as the intellectual heir of de Gaulle.[15] Under Pompidou, France continued to distance itself from American foreign policy. The Americans had hoped that Gaullism would die with de Gaulle, and President Nixon tried to woo Pompidou back into the fold. Pompidou, however, made it clear that although France was a friend of the U.S., it would not be a part of NATO or anything like it.[16]

V. F. Davydov reasoned that Nixon's first state visit with a European leader was with Pompidou because "France's independent foreign policy has long stood in the way of American imperialism.... Today American ruling circles have been forced to admit that future interatlantic relations depend to a considerable extent on France."[17] The Americans were persistent. They promoted the idea of the "Year of Europe" in 1973 in part to strengthen relations with France, but the French continued to resist American pressures toward Atlanticism.[18]

According to Soviet analysts, the French government under Pompidou promoted "Europeanism" as opposed to "Atlanticism" within Western Europe. In fact, a Soviet analyst noted in 1983 that the major new accent in French policy after de Gaulle was Pompidou's emphasis on "independent European cooperation."[19] The Gaullist impulse to deny U.S. "hegemony" by establishing European goals separate from American ones was a core stimulus to Europeanism. Although Europeanism did not become the official doctrine of the West European states, France actively promoted it as an alternative to American hegemony over Western Europe.[20]

As part of a quest for a separate political "space," France under Pompidou deepened its special relationship with the Soviet Union. In 1970, a Soviet writer noted that "scientific and technical cooperation has continued to expand, and military contacts have been established."[21] An article published in 1971 asserted that Soviet-French economic cooperation was deepening.[22] And by 1974, Soviet analysts were arguing that good Soviet-French relations were becoming a "vital need" for French policy.[23]

Under Pompidou, France also began to strengthen its relationship with the Arab world. French arms sales and economic ties to Arab nations increased, leading to conflict with the United States, which continued its close ties to Israel. As a result, not only did Pompidou continue de Gaulle's policy toward the Middle East, but "...in some instances went even further than de Gaulle."[24]

President Giscard d'Estaing (1974-1981)

Giscard d'Estaing continued to deepen cooperation with the other European states, creating a second phase of French security policy in which France moved closer to the concerns of its European neighbors. Giscard, unlike de Gaulle, worked effectively with the EEC, rather than condemning it as a supranational force undercutting French sovereignty. As an authoritative Soviet volume on France noted, "In contrast to the preceding period, when progress in development of the Community depended upon individual countries solving their national, especially economic, problems on a national basis, in the 1970s the ruling circles in France were forced to act in close cooperation with France's partners."[25] France faced a number of critical problems in the 1970s (such as the energy crisis and the monetary crisis) that required close collaboration with its EEC partners.

At the core of French cooperation with the EEC was the development of the Paris-Bonn axis to the West European "power center." The President of France and the Chancellor of West Germany were especially active in the 1970s in promoting economic and political cooperation between the two countries. According to V. P. Slavenov in his comprehensive analysis of the Presidency of Giscard d'Estaing:

> Bilateral ties and contacts between France and the FRG are being actively developed. Their ministers, bureaucrats, and businessmen are, you might say, meeting with each other on a daily basis. French and West German police and judicial organs collaborate very closely.... France and the FRG have more sister cities and broader cultural exchanges than do any other members of the Community. France's largest trade partner is the FRG and the FRG's is France; each one's share accounts for 20 percent of the exports of the other, which gives rise to close interdependence in their economic growth. Economic problems and especially attempts to find ways of combating inflation and unemployment, the state of affairs in the market, the stimulation of industrial production, the resolution of energy problems, and joint projects are in the center of attention at practically every high-level Franco-German meeting.[26]

The drawing together of French and German interests in Europe led to a strengthening of the West European power center. According to Slavenov, "...the politico-economic Paris-Bonn tandem, while remaining a driving force in 'European development,' has also become a main factor in the Community's opposition and resistance to attempts at an American diktat in the world and, especially, in economic affairs."[27]

Despite an emphasis on the European dimension in his foreign policy, President Giscard d'Estaing also reduced the level of tension with the Americans. There was a partial rapprochement of French and American policy. By the mid-1970s the United States and France were avoiding sharp confrontations with each other, for both sides needed to work together more closely to deal with the deepening "crisis of world capitalism." As G. Vorontsov characterized this change, "The departure of Paris in the second half of the 1960s from the one-sided focus on Washington and NATO allowed France greater room for manuever and led to sharp contradictions in American-French relations. France became the major political opponent of the United States in Western Europe. In contrast, during the 1970s, there were several signs of the well-known rapprochement between Washington and Paris."[28]

One such critical sign was the changing French stance toward U.S.-European security relations. Although continuing to insist on the primacy of its nuclear weapons as a force for independence, France embraced a closer relationship with the Western Alliance on defense issues. G. Vorontsov noted that Giscard d'Estaing signed a joint communique with the Americans in 1974, which stated that "cooperation between France and NATO is an important factor for ensuring Europe's security." This was "the first time in many years that such a statement had been signed by a French president."[29] Also, French military officials underscored the importance of NATO for French security. V. Slavenov noted the following:

Not long before his departure from the post of Chief of Staff of the Army, General de Boissieu appeared at the Institut des Hautes Etudes de Défense Nationale. He was forced to remind his audience that France had not withdrawn from NATO and that "contacts between the military staffs had never ceased, since General de Gaulle had decided to retain or establish delegations and liaison officers to the major NATO commands." Within the system of the NATO "defense of Europe" the French armed forces are located in the reserve, General de Boissieu stated.[30]

Soviet analysts have concluded that by the mid-1970s France's military posture had clearly changed. According to T. Sulitskaia, "...beginning in 1975 Paris implemented a number of serious compromise measures that were aimed at stabilizing its ties with the NATO military organization."[31] Prominently mentioned was the French Navy's participation in NATO naval maneuvers. French doctrine also changed. As T. Sulitskaia commented:

[There has been] a change in French military-strategic concepts since 1976. The essence of this concept, the so-called "doctrine of expanded security zones," consists in the fact that in the event of a conflict between NATO member countries and the socialist countries, the French armed forces could be immediately flung into the battle against the socialist countries at a "forward line of defense," i.e., on the borders of Czechoslovakia and East Germany.[32]

A. Kovalev noted statements by General Méry, the French Chief of Staff, that implied change in French doctrine. "For the first time in the 18 years of the Fifth Republic's existence it was declared that the French armed forces would participate in a 'battle'...according to the NATO concept of the 'advanced line of defense,' which France had refused to adopt until just recently."[33]

Especially indicative of France's changing position in the East-West military competition was the promulgation of the Military Program Law of 1977-1982 and its implementation by the Giscard administration. France planned a significant nuclear modernization. Kovalev noted the following:

At the end of the 1970s, France somewhat increased its emphasis on nuclear forces, whose modernization and improvement comprise the essence of the law adopted in fall 1979, which made clarifications in the 1977 military program designed for 1977-1982. The fifth nuclear-missile submarine was launched. Starting in 1985 the five submarines will begin to be (re)fitted with M-4 missiles. The French government has set itself the objective of having more than 600 nuclear warheads in another 10 years, which will be deployed on submarines and are capable of being independently targeted, like the American MIRV missiles. New models of missiles, new types of strategic aircraft, etc., are being elaborated.[34]

In spite of the partial rapprochement in French-American relations, tensions remained. France wished to use its improvement of relations with NATO to strengthen the West European power center. The Americans simply wished to reassert Atlanticism in a new form, namely, "interdependence" or "trilateralism."[35] France's efforts to strengthen West European independence were seen to lead "inevitably" to confrontation with the United States.[36] The United States could no longer rely on Atlanticism to dominate Western Europe. The West Europeans now realized that they "were an important component of the 'security' of the Americans," according to Iu. Davydov.[37] This realization provided the West Europeans with more room for maneuver with the Americans. As V. Shein noted, "Washington cannot disregard such strong tendencies in the allied countries as, for example, the determination of France (which could not, after all, be 'driven back' into the NATO military organization), above all, and of the Federal Republic of Germany to conduct a more independent policy...."[38]

For Soviet analysts, a critical dimension of French independence continued to be France's policy of detente toward the Soviet Union. Annual French-Soviet summit meetings were held throughout the Presidency of Giscard d'Estaing.[39] One Soviet analyst went so far as to suggest that French influence within the West European power center was due largely to its "realism" in dealing with the Soviet Union. Iu. Davydov argued that France's political prestige "grew not so much because it had become a nuclear power as because it was the first major West European country to acknowledge many realities of post-war Europe."[40]

As U.S.-Soviet relations worsened in the late 1970s, France was seen as an important "bulwark" for detente in Europe. When Iu. Davydov argued that Western Europe and the United States had developed different "interests" in detente, he had in mind the role of France in maintaining the European interest in detente.[41] By the "early 1980s France and the Soviet Union had solid experience in fruitful cooperation in the interest of peace."[42] Similarly, it was noted that as the Americans and NATO developed plans to heat up the arms race in Europe by deploying new American missiles, Soviet-French relations provided "an example of stability and accord."[43]

Nevertheless, all was not rosy in Soviet-French relations. As early as 1976, at least one Soviet analyst noted the development of opposition to detente in French policy. According to Y. Vladimirov,

> It was no accident that France's withdrawal from the NATO military orgnization evoked a strong opposition on the part of the pro-Atlanticist forces inside and outside France, which are still dreaming to return France to NATO's fold and simultaneously to hamper the development of Soviet-French cooperation. Of late the struggle concerning the stand made by France with respect to NATO has become especially sharp. Fresh impulse was given to it by the statement made by General Guy Méry...that in case of a military conflict between the NATO countries and the socialist states of Europe the French troops will take part in the battle of an "advanced defense line."[44]

This Soviet article clearly linked detente with the classic policy of Gaullism in security policy. The changes in French policy introduced by Giscard d'Estaing designed to increase France's role in European security were seen by the Soviets as basically incompatible with detente.

President Mitterrand (1981-   )

The defeat of President Giscard d'Estaing in the 1981 election was due, in Soviet eyes, to the economic difficulties confronting France.[45]

It was expected that the new government--an alliance until July 1984 of the French Socialists and Communists--would continue the "positive" elements of President Giscard d'Estaing's policy, namely, the special relationship with the Soviet Union. Detente would be bolstered in the difficult times of the early 1980s by the continuation of the special relationship.

Instead, France toughened its stance towards the Soviet Union and departed from the detente policy of the past. This change occurred, at least in part, because the French Socialist party made compromises with the French bourgeoisie at the expense of "genuine" cooperation with the French Communist party.[46]

A good sense of the Soviet view of the deterioration in French foreign policy was provided by the special correspondent of the Institute of the World Economy and International Relations in France, A. Kudriavtsev. Although French officials continue "to repudiate decisively the possibility of France's returning to the NATO military organization, at the same time they emphasize allegiance to allied duties."[47] The Mitterrand administration has interpreted as part of its "allied duties" the propagation of the line that the Soviet Union has gained a "military edge" in Europe. Mitterrand has called for "more arming to strengthen the U.S. nuclear guarantee" by supporting the deployment of U.S. Pershing IIs and cruise missiles in Europe.[48] But "...it is hard to understand how erecting a nuclear fence very near France's eastern borders will strengthen its security."[49]

Kudriavtsev contrasts the negative trends in French policy with the "real" needs of French security. "At present [French] experts reiterate that given a global nuclear-missile balance and tension in relations between the two 'superpowers,' strengthening the Atlantic bonds is turning into the sole and almost natural line of conduct for France. They have begun to maintain that counteraction against the mythical 'Soviet threat' must become dominant in the country's foreign policy...."[50] France's "real" security needs are quite different.

The real increasing danger to peace is gradually bringing ever broader social forces in France to understand that problems of security are not resolved by military means alone, to the detriment of political ones. In this connection, it is difficult not to agree with the thought expressed on the pages of *Le Monde*: "If there is someone among us today who is inclined to underestimate the results of detente, it is only because they are considered to be attainable once and for all." Meanwhile when the turn towards an increase in international tension took shape, French diplomacy's maneuvering potential, always noted for its flexibility, narrowed, and progress towards resolving a number of highly important problems was impeded. The normalization of the political climate in the world, and above all in Europe, is a task that meets the fundamental national interests of a strong independent France.[51]

Despite their hopes, the Soviets recognize that the concrete Franco-Soviet relationship has deteriorated. French officials have downplayed the Franco-Soviet economic relationship. The French government has also expelled Soviet officials in connection with charges of espionage. One Soviet official's reaction to the expulsion was to indicate that as a result France "has just destroyed the privileged position that it enjoyed in the panoply of Soviet foreign policy."[52] The French government, for the first time, clearly identified the Soviet Union as the military threat against which French forces are deployed in the Military Program Law adopted in late 1983.[53] The annual summit meetings between French and Soviet heads of state have been jettisoned by Mitterrand. When Mitterrand finally met with Soviet officials in Moscow it was occasioned by the most blatant presentation of Western interests on the human rights issue in memory.

Soviet analysts, however, still hope that France will reverse its drift into anti-Sovietism. As O. Lomov noted, "The massive campaign of anti-Sovietism and espionage that has engulfed France will not bring laurels to its initiators. The Soviets believe that the French have not forgotten with whom they have built a Europe of stability and security, or what Soviet orders in the framework of bilateral trade have brought, and are still bringing, the French workers when the unemployment rate is so high in France. Moscow is also convinced that France's real national interests lie in European cooperation and friendship with the Soviet Union, and not in confrontation."[54] Even after the June 1984 summit the Kremlin held out hope. "Washington has not succeeded in depriving its allies totally of their independence and their aspirations to consolidate their ties with the Soviet Union," an authoritative commentary in *Pravda* noted.[55]

The drift toward anti-Sovietism has been accompanied by a revival of Atlanticism. The main elements of this revival have been French support for the deployment of new U.S. nuclear missiles in Europe, greater cooperation with the Americans in military affairs, and a noticeable shift in the French doctrine of independence toward greater cooperation with NATO.[56]

The Soviets consider French support for the deployment of Pershing IIs and cruise missiles in Europe to be threatening to Soviet interests, even though none of these missiles will be deployed on French soil. S. Borisov noted that "The pro-Atlantic shift in the French government's political course cannot help but worry people."

He illustrated this statement by observing that "The present French leaders completely support the plans to deploy American nuclear weapons in Europe."[57] Iu. Erashov noted that under President Giscard d'Estaing, "France had adhered, in principle, to a neutral position; it believed that it was not directly affected" by the Euromissile decision since it had left the NATO bloc. In contrast, the support given by the Mitterrand administration to the INF deployment contradicts the traditional French position of independence.[58]

In addition, the French government, by refusing to allow its strategic forces to be included in the INF negotiations, has "objectively" supported U.S. interests. Soviet analysts have consistently underscored that French identification of the Soviet Union as the "threat" against which French missiles are directed, as well as France's continued adherence to the Western Alliance, means that French nuclear forces are part of the NATO potential. As N. Leonidov noted, "Does Paris's officially proclaimed 'independence' in nuclear facilities really change the targeting of the French missiles or make them less lethal? It is obvious to any sensible person that the French nuclear facilities...are a component of the North Atlantic Alliance's potential and must be taken into account at the Geneva talks."[59]

The Mitterrand administration is also perceived to have stepped up the level of direct military cooperation with the Americans. As A. Krivopalov, *Izvestiia's* correspondent in Paris, noted, "France is to take a more extensive part in NATO's measures and maneuvers. American nuclear submarines have been allowed to call at French ports. Planes from U.S. aircraft carriers can now overfly French territory and refuel in its air space. For the first time the Military Program Law has described the Soviet Union as the sole opponent of France. This has caused some of the commentators to ask: Is it accidental that the five-year French military program, providing for a considerable rise in the French nuclear arsenal, 'fits in' with the similar U.S. programs?"[60]

Soviet analysts have particularly noted the deepening cooperation between Bonn and Paris in security affairs. Paris has drawn closer to NATO in order to work more closely with Bonn, in the opinion of Soviet analysts.[61] The two countries have deepened their collaboration in military production, as in the plan to create a joint combat helicopter.[62] V. Baranovskii has argued that "...such cooperation between the two major continental powers can be the foundation for a West European military complex."[63] In fact, the strengthening of the Bonn-Paris axis in security affairs has been seen by Paris as a means for building greater European defense efforts within the West European Union (WEU). As Iu. Kovalenko noted,

> ...France intends to step up the implementation of plans to organize so-called "European defense" with the active participation of West Germany. The WEU, which unites seven European countries and in which Paris and Bonn play a decisive role, is to be its cornerstone. At the same time, France by no means counterposes "European defense" to the Atlantic Alliance. It is merely a matter of strengthening the "European nucleus" within NATO, certainly not of reorganizing the whole defense structure of the North Atlantic bloc.[64]

One dimension of Soviet concern about France's relationship with West Germany is the encouragement given to "negative" tendencies in West Germany. For example, France encouraged the WEU to lift the remaining restrictions on the joint production of offensive arms with West Germany.[65] Concern on this issue has been deep enough for the Soviet government to deliver an official protest to Bonn warning the West German government "to weigh carefully all those negative consequences that would inevitably arise" if Bonn uses the opportunity offered by the French-inspired actions to produce strategic aircraft or long-range missiles.[66]

Associated with the shift toward Atlanticism has been a shift in the French force posture. The basic alteration most noted by Soviet analysts is the formation of the Rapid Action Force (FAR). This is a newly formed, 47,000-man mobile force capable of being deployed from French soil to overseas areas or to the forward positions of NATO in the event of a European war. For the Soviets, the deployment of the FAR is inextricably intertwined with NATO's operations, at least in the European theater. As Iu. Buskin noted,

> The possibility of "concerted action" between the French units and the NATO forces in the center of the European Continent...has already become a reality. General de Llamby, to whom the mission of building the FAR has been entrusted, told journalists that from now on the question is one of elaborating jointly with the allies the "procedures for actions" for these forces in the European theater. In particular, the FAR will have access to the fuel and ammunition depots, including anti-tank missiles, on the territory of the NATO member countries. The question of ensuring the immediate transfer of FAR infantry units across allied territory has also been examined. Is it not greater than simply technical and tactical cooperation between French Army units and the armed forces of their NATO allies?[67]

In short, the departures from de Gaulle's policy of strict independence made by Giscard d'Estaing have been accelerated under the Mitterrand administration.[68] One Soviet analyst characterized France as having a "new defense strategy" under Mitterrand. There has been "...a switch from de Gaulle's 'omnidirectional defense' to 'defense in forward positions.' French statesman have talked much about France's indisputable membership in NATO and the consequent readiness to fulfill its allied obligations.... Defense Minister Hernu elaborated the concept of active military support for the allies from the onset of a crisis or conflict...."[69]

An excellent summary of Soviet thinking about the Mitterrand administration's security policy has been provided by Z. Arsen'ev in an article published in mid-1984. According to Arsen'ev, there has been intense action by France's "rightist" political circles to further strengthen Paris's ties with NATO, and the government has by and large cooperated with these forces.[70] The Atlanticists in France have seen many of their concepts implemented by the ruling Socialist party's leadership.[71]

While declaring that France does not intend to return to the NATO military organization, the French government has, at the same time, undertaken a whole series of actions that have introduced new aspects of its policy. There is the question, for example, of strenthening Paris's military cooperation with the other NATO countries, and primarily with the FRG. The French army is the largest one in Western Europe after West Germany's (about 550,000 men). Of them, approximately 50,000 are located on FRG territory and are viewed as a kind of second echelon for NATO. Recently they have been reorganized into "rapid action forces," expected to participate in joint actions with NATO troops "on the forward lines" in Central Europe.... In addition, the French units located near the FRG border will, in the coming years, be reinforced with new Hades tactical nuclear missiles, having a range of up to 450-500 kilometers, which are capable of inflicting a strike on the socialist countries' territory.

Judging from recent statements by Mitterrand, France is continuing to develop and test neutron weapons. Their production could begin in several months, or possibly, it has begun already. As Defense Minister Charles Hernu has acknowledged, this would signify a fundamental change in France's military strategy and a definitive transition to the position of the Atlantic strategy of "fighting on the forward line." After all, neutron weapons, like medium-range missiles, are primarily first-strike weapons and intended for offensive actions. They are necessary to those militant NATO circles who are relying on using nuclear weapons first.

The French press has noted that military cooperation between Bonn and Paris is experiencing a real boom. They also tie this in with the French proposal to remove the ban on FRG production of non-nuclear weapons, including long-range missiles and heavy bombers. Such a measure would be to the liking of FRG militarist, revanchist circles, but it patently contradicts the interests of security on the European continent. The Atlanticists are thereby undertaking more and more new actions aimed at drawing France into the groove of NATO's militant course step by step.[72]

Nonetheless, serious tensions remain in French relations with NATO. France continues to exercise full sovereignty over its nuclear weapons. France under Mitterrand emphasizes the primacy of nuclear weapons and, unlike the Giscard administration, has reduced the expenditures for conventional arms.[73] The heavy emphasis on the use of nuclear forces tends to weaken France's ties to the NATO bloc, observed one Soviet analyst.[74] Also, France continues to work against American hegemony in the Western Alliance and towards strengthening West European independence. This was evident, for example, when France rejected the American position in the dispute over the West European pipeline contract with the Soviet Union.[75]

In short, France remains an independent player in the East-West competition. France is shifting from the more dramatically independent position taken in the days of de Gaulle as it seeks to play a major role within the Western Alliance. Rather than rejecting the Western Alliance, the French are now perceived by the Soviets to be working against American interests in dominating the Alliance. The tensions between the French effort to strengthen the European pole of the Alliance and the U.S. effort to use its Western allies to implement American national security objectives will be of increasing significance in the years ahead. As Iu. Davydov has expressed this tension, "The U.S. has set for itself ambitious objectives that it doesn't have the resources for at the same time as Western Europe has determined that its foreign policy objectives must proceed from real, not imaginary, national (or regional) potentials."[76]

The French Force Posture

The Soviet view of the evolution of French security policy emphasizes both the relative independence of French policy and its significance for the Western Alliance. French policy is characterized as increasingly significant for the evolution of the Alliance as a whole. The significance of French security policy for the Alliance will be taken up in the next section. Here, the focus is on Soviet perceptions of the French force posture and its meaning in relation to French security policy. Put in other terms, how independent are French forces perceived to be, politically and militarily?

The core of France's policy of independence is its nuclear force. Soviet analysts have clearly noted the priority that nuclear weapons have for France. In rankings of missions for the various French forces, the nuclear mission is consistently ranked highest by Soviet analysts. For example, S. Rudas lists the major tasks confronting the French

Navy as the following: "Participating in the national nuclear-missile 'system of deterrence,' providing protection for national merchant shipping, and fulfilling the functions of 'showing the flag.'"[77] Similarly, Captain Volodin indicates that the main mission for French naval air forces is to "deliver strikes (including nuclear) against opponents' forces at sea and on shore, against shore targets, and to support SSBN combat patrols...."[78] The French Air Force is similarly considered to have nuclear missions as its priority. Not only is strategic aviation the premier arm of the air force, but French air defense forces are considered to have as their primary mission the protection of strategic nuclear force bases.[79] Only the army is given a more ambiguous mix of missions, with the nuclear mission much less clearly in command of resources.[80] The army is, however, trained to use, and to exploit the use of, tactical nuclear weapons.[81]

The deployment of nuclear forces by France is seen as a clear expression of its desire for independence. As A. Efremov noted in 1972, the "decisive" quality of nuclear weapons appealed to the French elite due to "historical experiences."

France's military doctrine, elaborated in light of its policy to create independent nuclear forces, has borne the mark of a whole series of factors. The failure of French military thought in the first period of World War II, manifested in the defensive concept of the notorious "Maginot line," did have its effect. Post-war French doctrine has focused on vigorous offensive action in which decisive types of modern weapons are to take part from the very first hour of the war.[82]

Soviet analysts perceive French nuclear forces, although an expression of a desire for independence, to be integral components of NATO's nuclear forces because of France's continued commitment to its Alliance treaties. As I. Koloskov noted in 1976, "Although serious contradictions have arisen between France and the United States and between France and NATO, the leaders of the Fifth Republic have never--even during the years of deteriorating Franco-American relations--cast doubt on their alliance with the United States and their participation in the Atlantic Pact."[83] France's solidarity with the Alliance was underscored frequently in Soviet commentary on the Euromissile crisis as a reason for inclusion of French forces in the INF talks. The judgement was made that France's strategic weapons are "essentially a component of NATO's arsenal."[84]

Militarily, the situation is more ambiguous. French forces have an independent cast in some respects. Most significantly, France exercises "full sovereignty" over the decision to use its nuclear weapons; that is, France can make an independent decision to use nuclear weapons.[85] France, unlike the United Kingdom, has developed its nuclear forces largely independently from the United States.

Nonetheless, Soviet analysts argue that France, to execute its nuclear strike, relies on NATO to some extent. As E. Arsen'ev noted, "France continued and still continues to cooperate with NATO's military organization. In particular, the entire French system of surveillance, warning, and communication necessary for servicing and possibly actuating the French nuclear forces remains closely connected with NATO's corresponding system."[86]

The military effect of a French nuclear strike would surely not be independent from the Soviet point of view. It is clear to Soviet analysts that France has targeted not only Soviet cities, but also military and administrative-industrial targets critical to any Soviet war effort. For example, Captain I. Volodin noted that the primary mission of the French Navy was "delivering nuclear strikes against the opponents' *highly important military and administrative-industrial targets....*"[87]

Soviet analysts consider French nuclear forces and the doctrine governing their use to have become less independent as French security policy has evolved. The classic position of de Gaulle seemed to lead to the following conclusion: "The possession of nuclear weapons determines French military doctrine, whose essence boils down to the fact that France's available potential is to be sufficient to prevent an attack on France...."[88] Soviet analysts are now less certain that there is a strict correlation between nuclear deterrence and the defense of French territory. In an authoritative treatment of French military doctrine, Captain Karemov and Colonel Semin argued that France has adopted its own version of the flexible use of nuclear weapons. Whereas before the mid-1970s French officials spoke of the use of strategic nuclear weapons in a massive response, since then they have talked of using nuclear weapons "in stages" as France's vital interests are threatened. "This proves the country's military-political leadership's readiness to use all available weapons, right up to strategic ones."[89] The significant enhancement of French nuclear forces in the years ahead is seen to be in support not of a massive retaliation doctrine, but of a doctrine of nuclear weapons used in stages. As an authoritative article in *Pravda* underscored:

The present French military doctrine for the 1980s and 1990s, which approximates American-NATO models, gives a partial answer to the question of what objectives a sharp buildup in the nuclear-missile might and the modernization of the armed forces pursue. The previous doctrine, elaborated after France left the NATO military organization, limited the use of nuclear weapons strictly to defending its own territory. For the doctrine being reviewed, it is now a matter of expanding the notion of France's "vital interests" beyond the limits of the country's territory.[90]

Whatever the ambiguities surrounding the question of the independence of French nuclear forces, French conventional forces deployed in Europe--even those on French soil--are seen to be an integral component of NATO. France's political commitment to the Western Alliance is perceived to have led to genuine cooperation between French conventional forces and those of NATO. For example, Marshal Ogarkov has stated that "in the past few years France has been increasingly departing from the known line of General de Gaulle, increasing in every way practical military cooperation with NATO, up to and including coordinating the operational plans of its armed forces with NATO's general plans."[91]

From the beginning of its independent policy, France retained close ties with NATO. V. Slavenov has noted that even after 1966 France continued its work in several NATO military committees, namely, the Military Agency for Standardization, the Supreme Allied Commander Atlantic Anti-Submarine Warfare Research Center, the Advisory Group for Aerospace Research and Development, and the NATO Air Defense Ground Environment System.[92]

France's military relationship with NATO has, however, deepened in the 1970s and 1980s. Most notably, the French armed forces have participated more frequently in combined exercises with NATO forces.[93] For example, the French Navy participated in the NATO naval exercise "Ocean Safari-83." The aim of the exercise was to develop an operation to control sea lines of communication. Several French ships participated, including the aircraft carrier *Foch*.[94] According to Soviet analysts, this particular exercise demonstrated that France was willing to permit the American Navy to use French airspace. France allowed U.S. Navy A-6E aircraft to refuel over French territory, the first time such refueling occurred since 1966.[95] For Soviet analysts there is a close link between the cooperation in military exercises and the increased salience of the Western Alliance to French security policy. As Captain I. Volodin has articulated this linkage: "The statement by the country's military-political leadership about its loyalty to its North Atlantic bloc allies, which is regarded by Western military specialists as direct support for NATO's military interests, is indicative of the increased participation of France's Navy in recent years in the combat and operational training of the NATO Joint Armed Forces."[96]

Soviet analysts note that the French Air Force and Army are also involved in frequent exercises with NATO forces. In an important article on the French Air Force published in 1982, Lieutenant Colonel A. Pavlov noted that "France is carrying out close cooperation with the North Atlantic Alliance, considering it to be one of the main conditions for ensuring the country's security."[97] Pavlov went on to argue that the air force is "closely" connected with NATO's operational planning.[98] Illustrative of Soviet thinking about the relationship between French conventional forces and NATO is a map of the main airfields of NATO appearing in a 1984 Soviet article. In the analyst's thinking, there was no reason to differentiate between France's airfields and those of NATO. In fact, they were all lumped together under the rubric of the "airfield network of the main NATO countries in Europe" (see figure 5.1).

In addition to participating in joint military exercises, France is taking a leading role in encouraging West European nations to promote indigenous armaments production. Although France is not a member of the Eurogroup component of NATO, France has become a key member of the Eurogroup committee dealing with armaments production. France participates in order to promote French arms sales, but the effect is to promote greater West European production of conventional arms, a trend not favored by the Soviet Union.[99]

French conventional forces do, however, have an important capability for independent action, especially outside Europe. Notably, the French Navy provides French leaders with an ability to project power and to exercise influence in Africa and the Middle East. As B. Kolker noted, "The existence of military bases on the territory of several French-speaking countries in Tropical Africa, on islands in the Indian Ocean and in the Mozambique Channel, on La Reunion Island and in the Republic of Djibouti, as well as its naval presence in the waters surrounding east and northeast Africa, make it possible for France to play an important role in resolving the problems of the entire African continent and the Arab East."[100]

But even French military actions outside Europe have a connection with the Alliance. Of the European NATO allies of the United States, only France and Britain have the real capability to involve themselves in "Alliance" military operations outside Europe. Soviet analysts have underscored that recent French actions in Chad and Lebanon have "encouraged" the Americans to seek greater Alliance cooperation in military actions beyond NATO's boundaries. With regard to Chad, V. Zorin has noted that "France, together with the U.S., in 1983 intervened militarily in the internal struggle in the

Source: Col. A. Alekseev, "The Airfield Network of the Main NATO Countries in Europe," *Zarubezhnoe voennoe obozrenie*, 1984, no. 1:65.

Fig. 5.1. The Main Airfields in the FRG, France, Italy, Belgium, and the Netherlands.

and have been concerned that operational cooperation might be transformed into sustained political cooperation outside Europe.

Based on Soviet perceptions of the French force posture, it is likely that Soviet military planners have reached the following judgements about French behavior in a future war in Europe. First, the probability that French forces will be involved in NATO's conventional operations is high enough that Soviet military planners must prudently plan to operate against them. Second, France will most likely use nuclear weapons to defend its territory; other uses remain much more problematic. Third, if the Soviets begin a full-scale war in Europe, they might well be willing to run the risk of trying to intimidate the French into not using their nuclear weapons during Soviet conventional operations. Soviet conventional forces would probably have a primary mission of degrading not only NATO nuclear weapons in the European theater, but French nuclear forces as well.[106] Soviet targets probably would include French ballistic missile submarines.[107]

The Political and Military Impact of French Security Policy

For Soviet analysts, the significance of French security policy lies in its impact on American and West European policy and in the subsequent positive or negative consequences for Soviet security policy.

The major political effect of French policy has been to stimulate the "Europeanist" tendency in Western Europe. A. Utkin has identified Europeanism as "...an ideology of isolating Western Europe, of forming the West European alliance as an autonomous center in the world arena."[108] Utkin emphasized that Europeanism has worked at cross purposes to Atlanticism. "Europeanism as an ideology focuses on greater independence from the hegemonic power of the capitalist world in the postwar period--the United States--which results in the definite anti-American trend of Europeanism."[109]

France has played a critical role in challenging American hegemony and in encouraging the emergence of Europeanism as a practical ideology guiding the formation of a more independent West European power center. V. Lukin has underscored the significance of the pioneering role of France in promoting Europeanism. Although Gaullist Europeanism was fairly superficial (in that it relied solely on nationalistic aspirations), "...there is scarcely any doubt that it was the Gaullist trend that played the decisive role in forcing Atlanticism into the background...and in breaking through the political surface of

Republic of Chad, which led to an intensification of conflict in Central Africa...."[101] This action was associated with the evolution of French security policy, which was permitting "a broadened sphere of action for the NATO bloc...."[102] Similarly, French actions in Lebanon have been seen as supportive of the American desire to act outside Europe with its NATO allies.[103]

For the Soviets, all that is required for a new "threat" to be established is for joint action to occur among the Alliance members. Soviet analysts are aware, however, that the Americans seek more than simply episodic joint actions. As V. S. Mikheev has noted regarding American policy:

> Congress pays great attention to the NATO allies' attitude towards American plans to expand the bloc's sphere of action. Although, as is noted in Congressional materials, the level of American-West European cooperation in Southwest Asia is "considerably higher than is usually assumed," since France and England have military ships in the Indian Ocean and military advisors in the region's key countries, with both states having forces analogous to the American "rapid deployment forces." Nevertheless, Washington wants much more: official commitments by its allies to take part, within the limits of NATO, in possible military conflicts far beyond Europe's borders or to compensate completely for the transport of American troops from the European theater to other regions of the world....[104]

Soviet analysts tend to assume that the Americans' insistence on formal commitments by France to participate in NATO actions inside and outside Europe will continue to create serious tensions with the French. The French desire to stay out of the integrated military command and the American desire to have France rejoin the command will keep providing the Soviets with hope that intra-Alliance tensions will continue to inhibit Alliance coordination.[105]

In summary, Soviet analysts view French military independence as best understood in terms of deploying and trying to protect and control an independent nuclear force. French conventional forces, however, are considered an integral component of NATO forces in Europe. Perceived changes in recent French security policy are seen simply to reinforce the basic judgement that French conventional forces are highly involved in NATO planning and operations in the European theater. French conventional forces outside Europe are seen as a major means for the exercise of influence in the Third World and hence a means to satisfy French aspirations for a meaningful role in global affairs. Soviet analysts do, however, note a "high degree" of cooperation between the American and French navies outside Europe the Europeanist attitude and practical initiatives."[110] The Gaullist course was a negative one in that it acted "primarily to destroy the old Atlanticist ideo-psychological and political stereotype."[111]

Europeanism as a trend and France's critical role in promoting it are seen as a two-edged sword by Soviet analysts. Europeanism is a positive trend to the extent that Atlanticism or American hegemony is undercut, but a negative trend to the extent that a West European power center emerges as a result. The significance of France's security policy is perceived as intertwined with the Europeanist trend.

French policy and the Europeanist tendency with which it is associated have undercut American hegemony. The withdrawal of France from the integrated military command means to the Soviets that French compliance with American policy can never be assumed by Washington. The French can operate as useful interlocutors between the Russians and the Americans or between the Russians and other West European states. From the Soviet point of view, it is better for France to be a "perturbator" in West-West relations than a consistent supporter of American positions.[112]

The withdrawal of France from the integrated military command has also had important consequences for U.S. military policy. First, the Americans have lost the "automatic" use of French territory in a war. Because France's geographical location is critical to the conduct of a conventional campaign in Europe, its unavailability to the integrated military command is seen as an important loss for the Americans.[113] Second, the French have consistently rejected the American doctrine of limited nuclear war. According to Soviet analysts, the Americans have planned to fight various forms of limited nuclear war, whereas the French plan for an all-out nuclear war.[114] The clear implication is that French nuclear forces seriously complicate American plans for exercising escalation control over Western nuclear forces. Third, the French example has encouraged other Western states, such as Spain, in the direction of only partial involvement in American warfighting plans.

Although the French policy of independence has yielded benefits from the Soviets' point of view, they nevertheless perceive France's role in strengthening a West European power center as a largely negative one. To gain some understanding of how Soviet analysts generally treat the nature, prospects, and challenges of the Europeanist tendency, the argument of one Soviet analyst is presented below. The work analyzed is a chapter by V. P. Lukin on the emergence of the West European power center in his 1983 book entitled *"Power Centers": Conceptions and Reality.*

Lukin first discusses the emergence of a West European power center in the economic sphere, where there have been objective shifts in the "correlation of forces" between Western Europe and the United States.[115] The political domination that the United States could exert over Western Europe due to American economic predominance has been weakened by the narrowing of the economic gap between the two power centers. "This means that the gap between the West European countries and the United States in the level of economic development, which, in the opinion of certain economists, took shape more than 100 years ago and assumed particularly contrasting forms after the end of World War II, has, on the whole, been abolished, and this fact could not help but have extremely significant political consequences."[116]

West European economic power, however, has provided only the prerequisite for the emergence of West European political power. A major force retarding the political emergence of Europe has been the continued military domination of Western Europe by the United States. From Lukin's point of view, the political emergence of Europe is inseparable from its emergence as a military power, even if firmly allied with the United States.

Stimulating the emergence of West European military power is the growing doubt about the American nuclear guarantee.

> Above all it is the effectiveness of the American guarantees on a global-strategic level that is subject to doubt by the West European allies. They are convinced that the Soviet Union's attainment of a position of approximate equality in this sphere in the early seventies has led to the fact that the probability that the United States will use its main "deterrent forces" in the event a military conflict breaks out in Europe has fallen to a minimum and cannot at the present time be recognized as a factor upon which the West European ruling circles could realistically base their expectations.[117]

The French heresy of the mid-1960s in casting aspersions on the American nuclear guarantee has become West European orthodoxy. "At the present time there is a slow, but quite definite process going on of pulling the 'West European rear' towards the position of the Gaullist vanguard of the sixties."[118]

At the core of a West European military power center would be greater military cooperation among France, West Germany and Britain. Lukin notes one form a broad division of labor within Western Europe might take:

> In particular, it is proposed to specialize their armies in such a way that the Bundeswehr will basically represent the conventional armed forces, focused

mainly on the European theater of operations. England and France have concentrated on providing the West European "nuclear umbrella," while France would, in addition, be granted the exclusive mission of foreign military intervention (primarily in the developing countries). In the nuclear sphere this project plans to return to the old idea of uniting French and British nuclear forces and of expanding the spheres of their potential operation so that they do not only "shield" the national territories of the two countries but, under certain circumstances, play the role of being a kind of "detonator" of a nuclear conflict.[119]

The Mitterrand administration is viewed as a major proponent of such a course of action for Western Europe. "Proof of the spread of these kinds of sentiments is the fact that after François Mitterrand came to power in France, they not only did not diminish, they became a component of the country's governmental course."[120] To support his contention, Lukin cites official French statements and the government's attempt to "step up the activity of the West European Union." France initiated a proposal in December 1981, which was adopted by the West European Union's Assembly, "to order the European Council to prepare the way that should lead to the creation of a European alliance based on the Treaty of Rome and the Brussels Treaty. This resolution, adopted by the majority...is an extremely important symptom, which gives proof of the move by the West European rear closer to the French vanguard. Broad support is gradually taking shape to include the military-strategic problems in the general current of forming a West European 'power center.'"[121]

Lukin is well aware of the numerous difficulties that confront the emergence of independent West European military power. First, Atlanticist tendencies remain strong in many parts of Western Europe. "Within the ruling circles of the West European states (especially in the FRG, England, and Italy) sentiments continue to remain strong that favor the improvement of American-West European relations in the military sphere in the Atlanticist mode."[122] Second, tensions among West European states weaken the trend toward greater strategic cooperation. There are critical tensions between France and Britain. "Sharp political contradictions between France and England have, until now, placed nuclear cooperation between them outside the limits of what is politically possible."[123] It is also difficult for the Europeans to resolve the problem of how to integrate West Germany into a West European military organization. "No less politically complex is the problem of the West German Bundeswehr's integration into the structure of European strategic planning."[124] Third, France's nationalistic tendencies, especially with regard to nuclear policy, tend to impede military integration. "The

French ruling circles' constant tendencies to combine West European group interests with French 'national interests' have also not been conducive to organizing the daring projects advanced in Paris on a practical basis."[125]

Nonetheless, "...in the long-term, the Europeanist power-center tendencies of Western Europe's ruling circles will, apparently, gradually gather strength and will be reflected in concrete political actions."[126] A good sense of Lukin's view of the current dynamics of the situation is evident in the following:

> On the whole, one can say that in the complex and contradictory process of forming a West European capitalist "power center," the military-strategic aspect lags considerably behind economic integration and politico-institutional coordination. Before the start of the eighties, this aspect was in an obviously embryonic state and had no serious practical significance. At the start of the present decade, however, the situation began to change appreciably. First, the discussion in West European countries on problems connected with elaborating a general European strategy have been noticeably intensified and stepped up. Second, one can sense the erosion of old "taboos" engendered by the inertia of movement during the more than 30-year period of American military-strategic domination. Third, discussions on possible scenarios for European integration in this sphere have been shifted to a high political level. Thus, in October 1982 the leaders of the two militarily strongest EEC countries--France and the FRG-- agreed to conduct regular (twice a year) consultations on security problems.
>
> And so, at the present time something like an intermediary status has taken shape, characterized by Gregory Treverton [former Deputy Director of the International Institute for Strategic Studies] in the following way: "America can no longer lead as it did, but Europe is not yet in a position to fill the gap."[127]

The sense that Atlanticism is in irrevocable decline and the relative independence of Europe on the rise is at the core of Soviet analyses of France in particular and of European security more generally. For Soviet analysts, Western Europe's independence can develop in one of two ways: Europe could become more independent militarily, or Europe could become more neutralist and embrace demilitarization.[128] There is little doubt which of these two alternatives the Soviets favor. Equally certain is that France is contributing to the emergence of the less desirable of these two alternatives for the Russians.

For some Soviet analysts, even the detente policy of the 1970s and early 1980s has had an ambiguous effect on the emergence of the West European power center. As an authoritative group of Soviet analysts noted, "...detente is capable, as it develops, of strengthening Eurocentric tendencies in the military policies of the West European powers, both within the framework of NATO and outside it. The

Europeanization of NATO, i.e., the increase in the relative importance within it of its European participants, may strengthen."[129] The dark side of France's detente policy has been noted by Sulitskaia. "The French government believed that the detente process had to parallel a strengthening of each West European country and all of Western Europe as a whole."[130]

Thus, the significance of French security policy to Soviet analysts is due largely to its contribution to the Europeanist tendency. Although France's example of independence has been important in stimulating the quest by West Europeans for greater independence from the Americans, France's contribution to security interdependence within the West European power center worries the Soviets more.

Soviet analysts have noted a number of ways that the evolution of French policy will decisively affect the emergence of security cooperation within Western Europe. First, to the extent that France develops its cooperation with Britain, a true European Nuclear Force (a Soviet term) could emerge.[131] Second, as the Franco-German security relationship becomes stronger, the Germans are more likely to acquire nuclear weapons, indirectly or directly.[132] Third, to the extent that the major West European powers, perhaps through the West European Union, cooperate in joint armaments production, the possibility of greater cooperation in conventional force deployments is enhanced. Standardization of arms enhances the probability of conventional military cooperation.[133] Fourth, the French example in using arms to gain influence in the Third World might well become the dominant tendency for the West European armaments industry. The Soviets have noted that France is already the number two arms producer in the capitalist world.[134] Due to the significance of arms sales for their own hard currency earnings, the Soviets might well be concerned with the growing threat to their arms markets posed by European armament producers.[135]

At least some Soviet analysts have posed the possibility that Atlanticism and Europeanism might not be polar opposites at all. Rather, Europeanism might provide the Americans with more room for maneuver in dealing with contingencies outside Europe. Actions taken by the Mitterrand administration to promote European cooperation and to reduce the anti-American thrust associated with traditional Gaullism are precisely a manifestation of something approaching a worst-case scenario for the Soviets. A particularly clear statement of the Soviet worst-case scenario was recently made by Captain V. Kuzar in the pages of *Red Star*.

Also aimed at increasing NATO's combat might is the idea--nurtured in certain circles of the European NATO countries and encouraged by the Americans--of creating a certain "triple alliance" within the bloc. In Washington they believe-- not without reason--that the so-called "independent West European defense," represented by the armed forces of France, England, and the FRG and subordinate, in the final analysis, to NATO headquarters, could be actively utilized in America's interests.

For their part, West German revanchist and militarist circles also see in the "triple alliance" the potential to consolidate their position in NATO and to seek a reexamination of the results of World War II. The FRG's revanchist elements are stepping up their activity given the deployment of American nuclear missiles in NATO countries that has begun and is continuing and given the intensification of the policy of militarizing West Germany, which is leading to a further destabilization of European security.

And finally, the strengthening of NATO's "European wing" would free the United States' hands even more for aggressive actions beyond the geographical framework of the bloc's "zone of responsibility." "Our alliance," declared Weinberger, "must plan possible actions beyond the boundaries of its region." But a number of NATO states are not only planning, but are already operating beyond these boundaries. In essence, the aggression against Lebanon has become an all-NATO one, carried out by "multinational forces," which have combined American, English, French, and Italian troops. Now Washington is trying to drag the NATO countries into joint operations in the Persian Gulf region.[136]

Besides contributing to the Europeanist tendency within the Western Alliance, French security policy has affected other areas of significance to the Soviets. One such issue is the effect of French security policy on Soviet arms control diplomacy. France's stance on arms control has been consistently negative from the Soviet point of view, with regard to both U.S.-Soviet bilateral agreements and the non-inclusion of French nuclear forces in any realistic forum.[137] The negative French stance is particularly harmful politically. It has undercut the ability of the Soviets to obtain a favorable agreement at the INF talks.[138] It impedes the ability of the Soviets to obstruct the modernization of the basis for a future European nuclear force, namely, the British and French nuclear forces.[139] It also has encouraged Chinese intransigence and has provided a basis for cooperation between China and France in developing strategic nuclear weapons outside the regulation of U.S.-Soviet arms control agreements.[140]

A second issue of significance to the Soviets is the effect of French security policy on Soviet military strategy. If the Soviets have made conventional warfighting their basic military option, then the importance of France in Soviet calculations should be growing.[141] The French nuclear force, especially as it is modernized, will be of such significance that the Soviets might well plan to target it very early in a European conflict. The Soviets could conceive of a range of conventional strikes against French land-based nuclear assets and strategic nuclear submarines. A recent Soviet map of French "Air Force facilities" looks quite like a target list for Soviet planners (see figure 5.2). It is very unlikely that the Soviets will want France to retain the option of escalating to nuclear weapons, thereby complicating or conceivably defeating their conventional warfighting strategy.

There is another dimension of the impact of French security policy on Soviet military strategy. The Soviets are paying a great deal of attention to the "coalitional" nature of any future European war.[142] Soviet emphasis is shifting away from studying simply the ability of the Americans to conduct combined NATO operations through the integrated military command and toward the ability of the Alliance to congeal politically in crisis situations. From this standpoint, the absence of France from the integrated military command of NATO is less significant than France's effect on the cohesiveness of the major powers in the Western coalition.

A third issue of significance to the Soviets is the effect of French security policy on Soviet policy in the Third World, especially in the Middle East. In light of the close ties that France has developed with the Arab Middle East, the Soviets now have to compete with both the Americans and the French if they are to reduce the Western presence in the region. U.S. reverses or difficulties in the region do not simply redound to Soviet advantage, for often the French, not the Soviets, are the beneficiaries of American difficulties.[143] French arms sales, especially in the aerospace industry, have frequently been at Soviet expense.[144]

In short, the significance for Soviet analysts of French security policy is its effect on American options and on West European possibilities. The French policy of independence and the nuclear force structure with which it is associated are seen to have been, and to continue to be, critical factors affecting U.S. military policy in Europe. French policy has weakened U.S. conventional options in Europe. It has also complicated the American ability to control escalation in a European war. French independence, however, challenges Soviet interests to the extent that French policy stimulates, and cooperates in, a process of interdependence among the major West European states. Insofar as Europe is better able to defend itself, the Americans are left in a more flexible position to act globally. And, as the

Source: Lt.Col. A. Pavlov, "France's Air Force," *Zarubezhnoe voennoe obozrenie*, 1982, no. 4:46.

Fig. 5.2. Main French Air Force Facilities.

French nuclear forces are modernized, they will become a more significant problem for Soviet military strategy.

Notes

1. For two treatments of the Soviet-French relationship that touch on issues discussed in this paper see Michael J. Sodaro, "Moscow and Mitterrand," *Problems of Communism* 31 (July-August 1982): 20-36; and Robert Legvold, "France and Soviet Policy" in *Soviet Policy Toward Western Europe: Implications for the Atlantic Alliance*, ed. Herbert J. Ellison (Seattle: University of Washington Press, 1983), 61-90.

2. B. Khalosha, "NATO: Krizis uglubliaetsia, ugroza ostaetsia," *Mirovaia ekonomika i mezhdunarodnye otnosheniia* [hereinafter *Memo*], 1966, no. 10:10.

3. V. Baranovskii, "Azimuty vneshnei politiki Frantsii," *Memo*, 1978, no. 7:154.

4. See, for example, the point of view expressed by O. N. Bykov in *Zapadnaia Evropa i SShA: Ocherk politicheskikh vzaimootnoshenii* (Moscow: Mysl', 1968), chap. 1.

5. I. A. Koloskov, *Vneshniaia politika piatoi respubliki: Evoliutsiia osnovnykh napravlenii i tendentsii, 1958-1972* (Moscow: Nauka, 1976), 122.

6. N. N. Molchanov, *General de Goll'*, 2nd ed. (Moscow: Mezhdunarodnye otnosheniia, 1980).

7. N. Komin, "Maiskii krizis piatoi respubliki," *Memo*, 1971, no. 3:140.

8. G. P. Chernikov and D. A. Chernikova, *Storonniki i protivniki franko-sovetskogo sotrudnichestva* (Moscow: Mezhdunarodnye otnosheniia, 1971), 39.

9. V. A. Zorin, "U istokov razriadki (Iz opyta diplomaticheskoi raboty vo Frantsii v 60-70-e gody)," *Diplomaticheskii vestnik, 1982* (Moscow: Mezhdunarodnye otnosheniia, 1983), 198-199.

10. A. Vladimirov, "Pagubnye posledstviia 'atomnogo shantazha,'" *Mezhdunarodnaia zhizn'* [hereinafter *MZ*], 1963, no. 7:138-139.

11. Zhan Kanapa, "Frantsiia: Militarizatsiia ekonomiki i politiki," *MZ*, 1963, no. 9:49, emphasis in original.

12. Col. A. Slobodenko, "Franko-amerikanskie spory o strategii," *MZ*, 1965, no. 1:72.

13. A. E. Efremov, *Evropa: iadernoe oruzhie* (Moscow: Mezhdunarodnye otnosheniia, 1972), 108.

14. For an interesting treatment of the tensions in de Gaulle's European policy see Iu. I. Rubinskii, ed., *Frantsiia* (Moscow: Mysl', 1973), 418-426. For a statement of the conflict within French ruling circles between aspirations toward detente and West European integration, see V. Rakhmaninov, "Soviet-French Relations and European Security," *International Affairs*, 1970, no. 11:33.

15. Iu. Rubinskii, "Frantsiia bez de Gollia," part 2, *Memo*, 1969, no. 10:87.

16. Iu. I. Rubinskii, "SShA-Frantsiia: 'Normalizatsiia' protivorechii," *SShA*, 1971, no. 3:55.

17. V. F. Davydov, "Novyi raund amerikano-zapadnoevropeiskikh konsul'tatsii," *SShA*, 1972, no. 2:71.

18. V. F. Davydov, "'God evropy'-God protivorechii," *SShA*, 1974, no. 3:74-79.

19. V. A. Zorin in *Vneshniaia politika kapitalisticheskikh stran* (Moscow: Mezhdunarodnye otnosheniia, 1983), 109.

20. A. I. Utkin, "'Atlantizm' protiv 'Evropeizma': Bor'ba kontseptsii," *SShA*, 1974, no. 4:30.

21. T. Vladimirov, "Factor of Peace and Stability in Europe," *International Affairs*, 1970, no. 8:96.

22. Iu. Vladimirov, "Soviet-French Cooperation: Steady Progress," *International Affairs*, 1971, no. 8:69-71.

23. A. Gorokhov, "The Line of Developing Friendly Cooperation," *International Affairs*, 1974, no. 5:10-15.

24. Iu. Rubinskii, "Frantsiia: V poiskakh osobogo kursa," *Memo*, 1973, no. 11:82.

25. Rubinskii, ed., *Frantsiia*, 344.

26. V. P. Slavenov, *Vneshniaia politika Frantsii, 1974-1981* (Moscow: Mezhdunarodnye otnosheniia, 1981), 112-113.

27. Ibid., 112.

28. G. Vorontsov, "Amerikano-frantsuzskie otnosheniia v 70-e gody," *Memo*, 1978, no. 8:27.

29. Ibid., 35.

30. Slavenov, *Vneshniaia politika Frantsii*, 56-57.

31. T. I. Sulitskaia, *Kitai i Frantsiia, 1949-1981* (Moscow: Nauka, 1983), 135.

32. Ibid.

33. A. Kovalev, "O nekotorykh aspektakh frantsuzskikh voenno-strategicheskikh doktrin," *Memo*, 1978, no. 4:120. Also see Col. G. Vasil'ev, "Voennye raskhody Frantsii na 1979 god," *Zarubezhnoe voennoe obozrenie* [hereinafter *ZVO*], 1979, no. 5: 24-25.

34. A. A. Kovalev, *Frantsiia na pereput'iakh mirovoi politiki* (Moscow: Mezhdunarodnye otnosheniia, 1983), 51-52.

35. A. I. Utkin, "Sovremennaia faza v amerikano-frantsuzskikh otnosheniiakh," *SShA*, 1975, no. 11:26-37.

36. S. Vorontsova, "SShA i Frantsiia: Sfery vzaimodeistviia i protivorechii," *Memo*, 1980, no. 11:61-62.

37. Iu. P. Davydov, "Kurs Vashingtona na napriazhennost' i Zapadnaia Evropa," *SShA*, 1980, no. 10:32.

38. V. S. Shein, "SShA i NATO v kontse semidesiatykh," *SShA*, 1979, no. 6:13.

39. Slavenov, *Vneshniaia politika Frantsii*, 213-215.

40. Iu. P. Davydov, "SShA-Zapadnaia Evropa i predely kompromissa," *SShA*, 1975, no. 6:35.

41. Davydov, "Kurs Vashingtona," 33-34.

42. Rubinskii, ed., *Frantsiia*, 343.

43. "Vazhnoe sobitie mirovoi politiki," *Memo*, 1979, no. 6:6.

44. Y. Vladimirov, "USSR-France: A Decade of Fruitful Cooperation," *International Affairs*, 1976, no. 8:53.

45. A. Kudriavtsev, "Frantsiia--politicheskie sdvigi," *Memo*, 1983, no. 9:84-92.

46. A. Kudriavtsev, "Frantsiia i real'nosti vnutripoliticheskoi zhizni," *Memo*, 1983, no. 9:84-92.

47. A. Kudriavtsev, "Frantsiia v mire--god spustia," *Memo*, 1982, no. 10:57.

48. Ibid., 58.

49. Ibid.

50. Ibid., 64.

51. Ibid.

52. As reported by Michel Tatu in *Le Monde*, 10-11 April 1983, 6.

53. V. Pustov, "Narastaiushchaia ugroza: Iadernye sily," *Krasnaia zvezda*, 31 January 1984, 3.

54. O. Lomov in *Le Matin*, 9 June 1983, 19.

55. As quoted by Michel Dobbs, *Washington Post*, 26 June 1984, A9.

56. For a significant overview of the Mitterrand administration's military policy, see Col. Iu. Erashov, "Opasnaia evoliutsiia voennoi politiki Frantsii," *ZVO*, 1983, no. 9:13-17.

57. S. Borisov, "Iadernye tuchi nad evropoi," *Kommunist Vooruzhennykh Sil* [hereinafter *KVS*], 1983, no. 22:81.

58. Iu. Erashov, "Zapadnaia Evropa v tiskakh NATO," *KVS*, 1983, no. 18:77.

59. N. Leonidov, "Chto proiskhodit s voennoi politikoi Frantsii," *Krasnaia zvezda*, 19 April 1983, 4.

60. A. Krivopalov, *Izvestiia*, 31 August 1983, 1.

61. Iu. Iakhontov, *Pravda*, 8 June 1983, 5; A. Grigoriants, *Izvestiia*, 4 March 1984, 4.

62. Iu. Karlanov, "Tsena indul'gentsii," *Pravda*, 28 November 1983, 5.

63. V. Baranovskii, "NATO: EES v politike imperializma," *Memo*, 1984, no. 6:37.

64. Iu. V. Kovalenko, "Kuiut os'?" *Izvestiia*, 4 March 1984, 4.

65. Maj. V. Nikanorov, "Indul'gentsiia militarizmu," *Krasnaia zvezda*, 18 May 1984, 3.

66. *Washington Post*, 13 July 1984, 1.

67. Iu. Buskin, "Jaguars Approach the Target," *Moscow News*, 18 December 1983, 7.

68. For a Soviet statement that identifies 1976 as the turning point see P. Cherkasov, "Tendentsii atlantizma," *Memo*, 1982, no. 1:147.

69. C. Dadiants in *Sotsialisticheskaia industriia*, 9 July 1983, 3.

70. Z. Arsen'ev, "Frantsiia i kovarstvo kholodnykh vetrov," *Sovetskaia Rossiia*, 18 April 1984, 7.

71. Ibid.

72. Ibid.

73. Col. A. Gavrilov, "Voennyi biudzhet Frantsii na 1983 finansovyi god," *ZVO*, 1983, no. 6:24-26.

74. V. S. Mikheev, "Vashington-Parizh: Sovremennyi etap otnoshenii," *SShA*, 1983, no. 2:21.

75. T. V. Kobushko, *SShA*, 1982, no. 12:46-55.

76. Davydov, "Kurs Vashingtona," 31.

77. S. Rudas, "VMS Frantsii: Perspektivy razvitiia," *Morskoi sbornik*, 1977, no. 1:96

78. Capt. Volodin, "Aviatsiia VMS Frantsii," *ZVO*, 1981, no. 7:65.

79. Lt.Col. A. Pavlov, "Voenno-vozdushnye sily Frantsii," *ZVO*, 1982, no. 7:44.

80. Col. N. Frolov, "Sukhoputnye voiska Frantsii," *ZVO*, 1980, no. 11: 25-32; Maj. A. Simakov, "Ucheniia sukhoputnykh voisk Frantsii," *ZVO*, 1983, no. 3:34-35.

81. N. K. Glazunov and N. S. Nikitin, *Operatsiia i boi*, 3d ed. (Moscow: Voenizdat, 1983), 265-269.

82. Efremov, *Evropa*, 106.

83. Koloskov, *Vneshniaia politika piatoi respubliki*, 287. Also see Rubinskii, ed., *Frantsiia*, 359-361.

84. Erashov, "Opasnaia evoliutsiia voennoi politiki Frantsii," 14.

85. Rubinskii, ed., *Frantsiia*, 349.

86. E. A. Arsen'ev, *Frantsiia: Problemy i politika* (Moscow: Politizdat, 1978), 248.

87. I. Volodin, "Voenno-morskie sily Frantsii," *ZVO*, 1980, no. 9:59, emphasis added.

88. Slavenov, *Vneshniaia politika Frantsii*, 53.

89. Capt. Karemov and Col. G. Semin, "Voennye doktriny osnovnykh evropeiskikh stran NATO," *ZVO*, 1983, no. 7:17-18.

90. I. Shchedrov, "Mify i real'nost'," *Pravda*, 1 June 1983, 4.

91. N. Ogarkov, "Peace Must be Defended Reliably," *Soviet Military Review*, 1983, no. 12, suppl.: 17.

92. Slavenov, *Vneshniaia politika Frantsii*, 57.

93. Col. N. Frolov, "Vooruzhennye Sily Frantsii," *ZVO*, 1980, no. 8:10.

94. "French Participation in NATO Maneuvers Viewed," *FBIS Daily Report: Soviet Union*, 8 June 1983, G7.

95. V. Tomin, "Uchenie VMS NATO 'Oushn Safari-83,'" *ZVO*, 1983, no. 11:59.

96. Volodin, "Voenno-morskie sily Frantsii," 59.

97. Pavlov, "Voenno-vozdushnye sily Frantsii," 43.

98. Ibid., 47-48.

99. See V. Leushkanov, "Atlanticheskii generator vooruzhenii," *Memo*, 1978, no. 9:113-115; V. Naumov and Iu. Pokataev, "Evrogruppa NATO," *Voennye znaniia*, 1984, no. 4:31.

100. B. M. Kolker, *Afrika i Zapadnaia Evropa: Politicheskie otnosheniia* (Moscow: Nauka, 1982), 41.

101. V. A. Zorin in *Vneshniaia politika kapitalisticheskikh stran*, 129.

102. Ibid., 130.

103. "Evropa v mirovoi politike 80-kh godov," *Memo*, 1984, no. 2:9.

104. V. S. Mikheev, "Kongress i 'Atlanticheskoe partnerstvo,'" *SShA*, 1984, no. 2:69.

105. This judgement is reflected throughout S. B. Vorontsov, *SShA i Frantsiia: sopernichestvo i partnerstvo* (Moscow: Mezhdunarodnye otnosheniia, 1983).

106. This is the view, for example, of Charles Petersen of the Center for Naval Analyses. Also, Phillip Petersen and Maj. John Hines, *The Soviet Conventional Offensive in Europe* (Washington D.C.: Defense Intelligence Agency, 1983).

107. I. Kuz'min, "Shumnost' podvodnykh lodok i protivolodochnaia bor'ba," *Morskoi Sbornik*, 1982, no. 9:67-72. Kuz'min included French SSBNs in the list of Western threats to the Soviet Union that required an enhancement of Soviet antisubmarine warfare capabilities.

108. A. I. Utkin, *Doktriny atlantizma i evropeiskaia integratsiia* (Moscow: Nauka, 1979), 73.

109. Ibid.

110. V. P. Lukin, *"Tsentry sily": Kontseptsii i real'nost'* (Moscow:Mezhdunarodnye otnosheniia, 1983), 66-67.

111. Ibid., 67.

112. On the significance of the perturbator role, see Vorontsov, *SShA i Frantsiia*, esp. 83-89 and 113-121.

113. See, for example, Iu. Rubinskii, "Frantsiia i NATO," *Memo*, 1966, no. 12:27-28.

114. Mikheev, "Vashington-Parizh: Sovremennyi etap otnoshenii," 21.

115. For a fuller analysis of Soviet views on West-West conflict, see Erik P. Hoffmann and Robbin F. Laird, *The "Scientific-Technological Revolution" and Soviet Foreign Policy* (Elmsford, N.Y.: Pergamon Press, 1983), chap. 2.

116. Lukin, *Tsentry sily*, 69.

117. Ibid., 82.

118. Ibid.

119. Ibid., 85-86.

120. Ibid., 86.

121. Ibid., 86-87.

122. Ibid., 87.

123. Ibid.

124. Ibid.

125. Ibid.

126. Ibid., 89.

127. Ibid., 88-89.

128. See V. S. Shein, "SShA-EES: Uzel protivorechii," *SShA*, 1973, no. 1:63.

129. V. N. Shenaev et al., eds., *Zapadnaia Evropa: Ekonomika, politika, klassovaia bor'ba* (Moscow: Mysl', 1979), 261.

130. Sulitskaia, *Kitai i Frantsiia, 1949-1981*, 139.

131. For the fullest statement of the European nuclear force concept see V. F. Davydov, "Diskussiia o evropeiskikh iadernykh silakh," *SShA*, 1976, no. 3:28-38.

132. See, for example, V. Mikhnovich, "Raschety i proschety," *Krasnaia zvezda*, 14 June 1984, 3.

133. For a representative Soviet perspective on the West European Union see D. Proektor, "Kart-blansh perevooruzheniia," *Novoe vremia*, no. 19 (4 May 1984): 20-21. Also see Col. M. Ponomarev, "Pod diktovka Vashingtona," *Krasnaia zvezda*, 11 March 1984, 3.

134. I. Shchedrov, "Frantsiia i 'Pershingi,'" *Pravda*, 15 June 1984, 4.

135. See the argument contained in *Soviet Arms Trade with the Non-Communist Third World in the 1970s and 1980s* (Washington, D.C.: Wharton Econometrics Forecasting Associates, 1983).

136. V. Kuzar', "NATO-Al'ians vo imia agressii," *Krasnaia zvezda*, 8 April 1984, 3.

137. Slavenov, *Vneshniaia politika Frantsii*, chap. 7.

138. See, for example, G. Vorontsov, "Bezopasnost' Evropy i iadernoe oruzhie srednei dal'nosti," *Memo*, 1983, no. 12:17, 27.

139. Pustov, "Narastaiushchaia ugroza: Iadernye sily."

140. Sulitskaia, *Kitai i Frantsiia*, chap. 3.

141. On the shift in Soviet strategy to the conventional option see Robbin Laird and Dale Herspring, *The Soviet Union and Strategic Arms* (Boulder, Colorado: Westview Press, 1984), chap. 1.

142. See, for example, B. M. Khalosha, *Voenno-politicheskie soiuzy imperializma* (Moscow: Nauka, 1982).

143. See, for example, David B. Ottaway, "U.S. and France Compete in Persian Gulf," *Washington Post*, 25 April 1984.

144. See *Soviet Arms Trade*.

Conclusion

The basic political purpose of French nuclear forces is to ensure French independence. The difficulty is that the enhanced significance of French nuclear forces to the Soviets, the decline in Alliance cohesion, and the increased salience of West Germany to French security all call into question the meaning of independence if it is limited to the defense of French territory proper.

With the decline in Alliance cohesion, the contribution that France can make in strengthening the Alliance grows in importance. If France refuses to commit its nuclear assets to a European role, it can play that role only with its conventional forces. But if France continues the current trend of starving conventional forces to feed nuclear ones, France will weaken intra-Alliance relations, precisely when it needs to contribute more leadership to Europe, not hide behind its nuclear shield. Perhaps one way out is doctrinal--committing conventional forces more closely to NATO missions or to the forward defense of West Germany. This change would have to be made without reentering NATO's integrated military command, something that is beyond the pale in French politics.

West Germany can be the channel whereby France meshes its national interests with broader Alliance concerns. Many things that would be perceived in France as illegitimate in dealing with the Americans appear to be legitimate in dealing with the Germans. France seeks a bigger role for Europe in the Alliance, not the revitalization of American leadership over Europe through the Alliance.

However difficult the dialogue may be, the Franco-German security relationship is at the heart of any Europeanization of the Alliance. This dialogue is critical for defining the missions of French conventional forces in Europe, for solving certain military procurement problems, for more efficiently using defense resources, and for determining the optimal military role for French tactical nuclear weapons. The French have indicated that they intend to use tactical nuclear weapons only as a "final warning" of the intention to use strategic weapons. Even if this is so, the only actions the Soviets might consider a final warning would also be militarily effective and meshed, however loosely, with NATO.

Nonetheless, to move beyond a commitment to national independence defined strictly in terms of using nuclear weapons to defend French territory might well erode the French defense consensus. The breadth of the consensus to deploy nuclear weapons is evident. Its fragility is less so, but rests in the inability of French policy-makers to confront directly the broader European concerns bound up with the modernization of French nuclear forces. A possible erosion of the domestic defense consensus by a France trying to define a broader role for its nuclear weapons might well lead to a decreased public commitment to defense and thence to reduced defense spending.

Hence, French policy-makers face a central dilemma--the need to expand the concept of independence to encompass greater interdependence within the Alliance versus the need to maintain the myth that nuclear weapons serve only to "sanctuarize" French territory, this myth being central to the French defense consensus.

This dilemma will intensify as the Americans, Germans, and Soviets, each in their own way, place greater pressure on France to "compromise" its independence. The Americans hope that France will play a greater conventional role and increase the credibility of NATO's conventional deterrent. The Germans hope that France will play a greater conventional role and recognize a European role for its nuclear, especially tactical nuclear, forces. The Soviets insist that France is playing a key role in NATO and that French nuclear forces should certainly be counted as part of the Western deterrent.

The French for their part will continue to insist on the validity of their independent nuclear deterrent. Nevertheless, as French nuclear forces become more important to the credibility of Western defense efforts, it will become increasingly difficult for France to maintain its independent identification. There is no easy way out of this dilemma, a dilemma that the Soviets hope to exacerbate.

For the Soviets, the military significance of the French nuclear modernization program is three-fold. First, there will be a dramatic increase in the number of warheads that the French can use to strike Soviet territory. The Soviets will undoubtedly have an even greater incentive than they do now to prosecute and destroy French SSBNs in a wartime setting. Second, the French are creating another decision-making center in the Western Alliance that can execute nuclear strikes against Soviet military forces in Eastern Europe. Such a French capability clearly will complicate Soviet attempts to control escalation in the European theater. Third, if the Soviets do not significantly enhance their ballistic missile defense capabilities, France will begin to have limited counterforce options as its number of warheads increases.

The political impact of French security policy on Soviet interests has been ambiguous. To the extent that the Soviets are preoccupied with their rivalry with the United States, French policy has worked to Soviet advantage in certain respects, but perhaps not so in the long run. Insofar as the Soviets are concerned with the emergence of a polycentric world, in which the major powers of various regions might be arrayed in an "anti-Soviet" coalition, French policy might well be a stimulant in the emergence of a worst-case scenario. Not only might the Soviets face a globally assertive superpower, but they may also have to confront regionally assertive powers in Europe and Asia allied with that superpower.

A France assertive of its national interests through its independent force structure, yet still strongly allied to the United States, might well be the harbinger of difficult times for the Soviet Union as the global system evolves toward multipolarity. The Soviet Union might well have been more successful competing in a bipolar world.

Appendix A

"American Policy in Conflict With the Realities of Military-Strategic Equality"

Excerpts

Aleksei Arbatov, "Amerikanskaia politika v stolknovenii s real'nostiami voenno-strategicheskogo ravnovesiia" [American policy in conflict with the realities of military-strategic equality], chap. 7 in *Voenno-strategicheskii paritet i politika SShA* [Military-strategic parity and U.S. policy] (Moscow: Politizdat, 1984), 284-297. Excerpts translated by Susan Clark.

Parity and the Problem of Limiting Nuclear Arms in Europe

It is commonly known that military-technological differences in the strategic potentials of the USSR and the USA are also supplemented by the geostrategic asymmetry between the two powers. The latter consists in the fact that the United States--unlike the USSR--is capable of delivering a nuclear strike deep into the territory of the other side not only by means of strategic intercontinental arms, but also by utilizing forward-based and medium-range nuclear means deployed near Soviet territory.

This geostrategic asymmetry is of enormous importance in objectively analyzing both the military correlation of forces and the task of a dialogue on arms limitations that is very often ruled out by bourgeois specialists. For a thermonuclear war can be unleashed not only by a first strike of strategic forces, but also by using tactical and medium-range nuclear weapons in one of the theaters of military action [TVDs]....

This [geostrategic asymmetry] is why, given military-strategic parity between the USSR and the USA, during negotiations to substantially reduce its level, the problem of limiting nuclear weapons on a regional scale--primarily in the European TVD where the destructive potentials, the most powerful in mankind's history, of the two coalitions of states directly oppose each other--acquires very important significance. The whole danger of deploying the 572 new American medium-range missiles (Pershing IIs and cruise missiles), let alone the concrete destabilizing military-technical characteristics of these weapons systems, is also due to this. The geostrategic factors and the clearly pronounced properties of these missiles as first-strike weapons make the negative consequences of their deployment much greater than the purely quantitative addition of these means to the U.S. strategic arsenal. As a rule, bourgeois politicians, experts and journalists confine themselves to a [quantitative] appraisal. The extraordinary importance accorded to an agreement on this problem at the Geneva talks is stipulated by these [two factors].

NATO's "dual decision" of December 1979, as we recall, was and is justified by the "need" to strengthen American nuclear guarantees to the North Atlantic pact. It is maintained that whereas in the fifties and sixties the United States' massive nuclear superiority in strategic arms and nuclear means in Europe compensated for NATO's alleged lag behind the Warsaw Pact in general-purpose armed forces, in the seventies and eighties the situation has changed. Parity has taken shape between the USSR and the USA at the strategic arms level, while in nuclear weapons in the European theater the Soviet Union has ostensibly achieved "superiority" mainly owing to the deployment of new MRV mobile medium-range ballistic missiles since 1977, called SS-20s in the West. It is accordingly declared that the "sole way out" for NATO is to "additionally arm"--to build up U.S. nuclear means on the European continent....

On a broader plane the entire approach of the West's ruling circles to the so-called problem of the U.S. nuclear guarantees is untenable. There can be no doubt that a wide-scale military conflict between the Warsaw Pact and NATO would unavoidably evoke the use of nuclear weapons and would evolve into a global thermonuclear war. Such is political reality; it has been present for the last 40 years and will be retained into the future, regardless of certain partial changes and disproportions in the military correlation of forces. And it is namely the balance between the USSR and USA in strategic arms, between

East and West in nuclear means and general-purpose forces in Europe, that makes the provocation of such a war improbable. At the same time, by opening up the possibility of radically limiting and reducing the level of military confrontation and of easing political tensions, this "three-ply" equilibrium makes it possible to lower even further--and in the future to completely eliminate--the danger of World War III being unleashed on the European continent. Inasmuch as it is a question of guarantees of U.S. participation in such a war if it were nevertheless unleashed, they are fortifying themselves with the presence of about 300,000 U.S. servicemen in the European theater, with 7,000 nuclear warheads on various U.S. carriers deployed here, and with an enormous quantity of their arms and various kinds of combat equipment. Finally, its extensive economic, political, and ideological interests in Western Europe are extremely important to the U.S.

If all of this is not enough for the reliability of U.S. commitments to NATO, the 600 new American missiles on the continent are not capable of "correcting" the situation. If it is maintained that the U.S. will not risk using its strategic forces during the escalation of a possible European conflict, fearing a retaliatory strike against American territory, then what will the new U.S. missiles in Western Europe change?...

The Reagan administration has hastened to pass off the stationing of its missiles begun on the European continent as "an outstanding success" of U.S. and NATO policy and, secretly rejoicing in the failure of the dialogue, it began to hypocritically call for the Soviet Union to return to the negotiating table. There is no denying that the U.S. actions have created a danger of disrupting military-strategic parity; they have sharply increased the nuclear threat to the security of Europe and the entire world, and they have exacerbated international political tensions. But nevertheless, if one looks not at external manifestations but at the essence of what has taken place, it becomes clear that Washington has no foundations for celebrating a victory. Granted the United States has now been able to begin stationing its missiles in West European countries, but the political cost of this action was exceptionally great. When considering how large a gamble NATO made in implementing the resolution of the bloc's Brussels session of 12 December 1979, one must not forget how much the enormous political capital, the unheard-of strain on allied relations, and the unprecedented growth of anti-American and anti-nuclear sentiment in the general European public have cost in the subsequent 4 years in order to make this resolution a reality. If one recalls how relatively quickly and painlessly the American Jupiter and Thor medium-range ballistic missiles were deployed in Europe at the end of the fifties (they were removed in the first half of the sixties), then the scale of the political changes that have taken place in the world become quite apparent. Moreover, the initiated deployment of American missiles still does not mean that this question is definitively and irrevocably closed. In Western Europe the massive anti-missile movement is expanding, and the realistically thinking representatives of their ruling circles cannot help but take into consideration the growth of the direct threat to the security of the West European states. And here lies the deep contradiction between the interests of Washington and its allies on the Atlantic's other shore.

In a military-strategic respect the situation gives even less grounds for optimism for the supporters of nuclear superiority in the West. The American medium-range ballistic missiles deployed at the end of the fifties and the medium-range bombers and forward-based means the United States possessed substantially exceeded all Soviet intercontinental means for a retaliatory strike, to say nothing of the enormous superiority of U.S. strategic nuclear might and the still-remaining extremely low accessibility of U.S. territory to the other side's nuclear weapons. Given the present correlation of forces and the Soviet potential to take rapid and effective retaliatory measures, the new 572 medium-range American missiles cannot present the United States with its lost superiority either in the quantitative level of nuclear arms or in the capability to inflict a "disarming" or "decapitating" nuclear strike on the USSR....

Appendix B

"The Growing Threat: England's and France's Nuclear Forces in NATO's Plans"

Excerpts

V. Pustov, "Narastaiushchaia ugroza: Iadernye sily Anglii i Frantsii v planakh NATO" [The growing threat: England's and France's nuclear forces in NATO's plans], *Krasnaia zvezda* [Red Star], 31 January 1984, 3. Excerpts translated by Susan Clark.

The numerous organs of the West's enormous propaganda machine, which usually present a united position, are admitting a striking dissonance in their appraisals of the English and French nuclear forces. This fact is highly noteworthy since the stubborn U.S. refusal to count these forces in the overall balance of medium-range nuclear weapons in the European zone has become one of the reasons for the failure of the nuclear arms limitation talks in Europe. The unsubstantiated statements by official Washington, and at the same time by London and Paris, that the English and French nuclear potentials are supposedly designed only for national defense purposes, are independent and, owing to their limited size, cannot--so they say-- represent a threat to the USSR, have been clearly refuted by the unwilling admissions of a number of American and other NATO newspapers and by factual data cited by military specialists.

What kind of genuine independence can there be if, given a large- scale war, the British nuclear forces "would be," as the *New York Times* has stated, "immediately integrated into NATO"? The independence of France's nuclear forces has also been questioned, for example, in a report recently prepared by the Congressional Research Service. "The fact of whether France will participate in the NATO military organization is not of serious significance," the document notes. "The treaty on the creation of NATO engages France to the same extent as it does the other countries who signed it." One of the authors of the report, Charles Gellner, discusses the probable "existence of a definite coordination or exchange of information when the targets for the French nuclear weapons are selected." Because of this, as well as because of the fact that France's strike forces represent the third most powerful nuclear arsenal in the world, they "are becoming," the *Christian Science Monitor* concludes, "an important factor in any scenario for a war in Europe." Finally, General Rogers himself--the Supreme Allied Commander, Europe--has declared that in the event of war, France will add its forces to the Atlantic Alliance's forces "very quickly."

Once in a while during discordant discussions there can be heard revelations smacking of saber-rattling, this time the rattling of nuclear sabers. "France has a formidable nuclear arsenal," proclaims the *Washington Post*. According to the newspaper's facts, taken from top secret American intelligence documents, the French nuclear missiles are "capable of annihilating a minimum of 30 major Soviet cities." In the words of one American military specialist "the Russians will always have to take this factor into consideration." Scarcely-veiled threats resound from time to time on the British Isles as well. Even a few years ago, England's government pointed out in the *White Paper* that its nuclear forces, being an "inseparable part" of NATO's nuclear potential, "are capable of inflicting so much damage on the Soviet Union that the Soviet leadership has to take them into account."

Naturally, the Soviet Union cannot fail to take this into consideration. And, being guided by interests of its security and the security of its allies and friends, it is, quite naturally, demanding that the English and French nuclear forces be counted when determining NATO's nuclear potential in Europe.

As is well known, England's and France's nuclear weapons--aimed at the Soviet Union and the other socialist countries--represent an extremely imposing force. They make up one quarter of NATO's nuclear potential in Europe and now number more than 200 carriers, including 162 missiles with 420-430 nuclear warheads, each of these warheads having a yield ten times greater than the American atomic bomb dropped on Hiroshima.

The British fleet has four nuclear-powered submarines carrying 64 Polaris ballistic missiles, each with three warheads. They are now being replaced by improved missiles having six warheads each. The Conservatives' government has decided to replace the present missile-carrying submarines in the future with new, more powerful ones and to purchase Trident-2 missiles for them from the U.S. This missile will be many times superior to the Polaris missile in range (11,000 kilometers), in its circular error probable (90 meters), and in the number and yield of its warheads (7 warheads of 600 kilotons or 14 warheads of 150 kilotons each).

The modernization of the French nuclear arsenal is also being carried out at an accelerated pace; it is, in the words of the Minister of Defense, Charles Hernu, "the foremost of foremost tasks." At the present time, the French nuclear strike forces include 98 single-warhead ballistic missiles (80 of them on board the five nuclear-powered submarines and 18 in silos on the Albion Plateau in southeastern France), as well as 46 Mirage IV nuclear-missile-carrying bombers.

Next year they plan to commission a sixth nuclear-powered submarine, which will carry the new M-4 missiles having six reentry vehicles and capable, so Paris declares, of destroying an area 350 by 150 kilometers. The M-4 will have an improved range--up to 4,400 kilometers. Later on, they also contemplate using these missiles to arm four of the first five nuclear-powered submarines that are in operation. Thus, the number of nuclear warheads on French submarines will increase from 80 to 176 in 1985 and will grow even more in the early nineties when the seventh submarine is commissioned--the first of the new generation of nuclear-powered, missile-carrying submarines.

As for the ground component of the French strategic forces, all 18 S-2 missiles having a 150-kiloton yield are being replaced by improved S-3s, each with a megaton warhead and a range of more than 3,000 kilometers. Steps are being taken to further harden the silos in which these missiles are deployed.

The West is also paying attention to France's impending development of the new Hades missile with a nuclear warhead. Nor has it been ruled out to outfit it with a neutron warhead. Paris has officially stated that from 1984 to 1988 work will continue "on improving higher-radiation weapons," that is, neutron weapons. The range of the Hades missile exceeds 350 kilometers, that is, it is more than double that of its predecessor missile, the Pluton. And this means that, launched from Eastern France, the Hades could hit targets in the GDR and Czechoslovakia.

The might of the third component of the French nuclear forces--aviation--is also being constantly built up. Work is going on to re-equip the Mirage IV planes: starting in 1985 they will be outfitted with "air-to-surface" nuclear missiles, with a range of 200 kilometers. In addition, it is envisaged to bring in new, improved Mirage 2000 planes, capable of carrying nuclear weapons. They plan to order 165 such aircraft, as well as a new nuclear-powered aircraft carrier. In announcing this, Hernu declared that "air supremacy is the key to a war today."

An analogous process can be observed in England too. To supplement existing multi-purpose aircraft, the new fighter-bomber Tornado is joining the inventory; it is also designed to carry nuclear weapons. Additional squadrons of these planes are already being formed; seven of these squadrons will be based in the FRG, that is, near the borders of the socialist community countries; and two squadrons will be on the British Isles.

Thus, according to estimates by Western experts, by 1990 England and France will have up to 1,200 nuclear warheads. And according to the *Washington Post,* by that year the "French and English nuclear forces will be improved such that their systems will be in a position to hit up to two thousand of the opponent's targets." The fact that the opponent is implied to be the Soviet Union and its allies is openly discussed in London, in Paris, and, of course, in Washington. There they also make no secret of the fact that the strategic plans of these three countries are based on a refusal to follow the USSR's example to pledge not to use nuclear weapons first, as well as on a widely publicized intention to launch these weapons by surprise....

Appendix C

" 'Eurostrategy' and NATO's Eurostrategic Nuclear Forces"

Excerpts

Colonel-Engineer I. Belov, " 'Evrostrategiia' i evrostrategicheskie iadernye sily NATO" ["Eurostrategy" and NATO's Eurostrategic nuclear forces], *Zarubezhnoe voennoe obozrenie* [Foreign Military Review], 1981, no. 10: 8-10. Excerpts translated by Susan Clark.

Just what constitute NATO's strategic nuclear forces in Europe at the present time?

As the foreign press reports, in the event of war, earmarked to be transferred to the disposal of the Supreme High Command of the NATO Joint Armed Forces in Europe are five American SSBNs (figure 1) [not reproduced], with Poseidon-C3 missiles on board (a total of 80 missiles with MIRVs--having 10 or 14 Mk3 warheads, each having a yield of 50 kilotons and a range of 4,600 kilometers). The magazine *NATO's Fifteen Nations* also attributes 170 (according to other reports--156) F-IIIE and F bombers--nuclear-weapon carriers stationed at American air bases in Great Britain (their range--2,400 kilometers) to the Eurostrategic forces.

Great Britain plans to transfer four Resolution-class SSBNs with Polaris-A3 missiles (a total of 64 missiles with 192 Mk2 warheads, having an equivalent yield of 200 kilotons each and range of 4,000 kilometers) and 56 medium-range Vulcan B-2 strategic bombers (figure 2) [not reproduced], 48 of which are in combat units (each such plane carries nuclear bombs and its range is 2,800-4,600 kilometers). The British government has made the decision to replace the SSBNs on hand by building in the nineties four or five new nuclear-powered, missile-carrying submarines armed with American Trident-1 missiles (each missile will have a MIRV--eight Mk4 warheads having an equivalent yield of 100 kilotons and range of 7,400 kilometers). Five billion pounds sterling are being allocated to implement this program. However, in the next few years it is planned to equip available Polaris-A3 missiles with new MIRV-class warheads, developed according to the Chevaline program.

The British government is hedging the transfer of strategic forces to NATO with the condition of "preserving higher national interests," which signifies its intention to reserve for itself the right to make the final decision, depending on the situation.

The U.S. and NATO leadership does not discount the French strategic forces, although France withdrew from the bloc's military organization in 1966. At the present time they consist of 18 launchers for intermediate-range S-2 and S-3 ballistic missiles (the S-2 missiles are being replaced by S-3 missiles, scheduled to be completed by the end of 1982). The S-2 has a 150-kiloton warhead (and range of 2,750 kilometers), while the S-3 has a megaton-type thermonuclear warhead (more than 3,000 kilometers). Also included in these forces are five SSBNs with 16 M-2 missiles on each (500-kiloton warhead, 2,400-kilometer range), which are now being replaced by M-20 missiles (a megaton-type warhead, range up to 3,000 kilometers). By 1985 it is proposed to commission one more SSBN, and it is intended to equip all of them with more powerful M-4 missiles with MIRVs (seven warheads each having a yield of 150 kilotons and range of 4,500 kilometers). Instead of the 80 warheads now on French submarine nuclear-missile systems, in 1985 there will be 672. The new French government is examining the question of possibly building another two SSBNs.

The foreign press reports that whereas at the present time Great Britain and France allocate one or two SSBNs for combat patrol, in 1985 France will be able to send up to three missile-carrying submarines for this.

France has 50 medium-range Mirage-4A strategic bombers, 36 of which are in combat subunits. Each of them carries a nuclear bomb (60 kilotons) and has a range of 1,200-1,800 kilometers.

In accordance with the resolution by the NATO ruling organs, imposed by the Pentagon, in 1983 it is planned to begin the

---

1. 2,500 kilometers according to other Western press information (ed.).

deployment of 108 new Pershing II missiles (range of 1,800 kilometers)[1] and 464 land-based cruise missiles (2,500 kilometers) in Europe....

The West European press has noted that the American strategic nuclear forces assigned to NATO will actually be employed not with the knowledge of the bloc's organs, but according to the U.S. President's orders, since the NATO Joint Armed Forces in Europe are permanently headed up by a U.S. general who is, concomitantly, the Commander-in-Chief of the U.S. Armed Forces in Europe and is, first and foremost, subordinate to the Pentagon and the President of the United States.

In regard to the prospects for developing the bloc's strategic nuclear forces in Europe, the foreign press reports that the ruling circles of the U.S. and North Atlantic Alliance intend to arm them by the mid-eighties with higher-yield nuclear warheads (megaton-type) and with MIRVed warheads. It is not ruled out that in the future European cruise missiles will become part of the inventory and the number of SSBNs will increase. *Among the participating countries the tendency is growing to create European strategic nuclear forces within NATO that are independent of the U.S.* [Emphasis added.] It is believed that the mid-eighties could signify a "new step" in the development of NATO nuclear forces in Europe.

Thus, although an official decision on creating NATO Euro-strategic nuclear forces still has not been made, they do, in fact, exist and are constantly being strengthened. Plans for their use pursue patently aggressive objectives and are aimed against the Soviet Union and the other countries of the socialist community. This obligates the Soviet soldiers to keep a vigilant eye on the imperialists' schemes and, in association with the soldiers of fraternal armies, to alertly stand guard over socialism's achievements.

Name Index